NEW MEXICO

ROUTE 66 ON TOUR

D0923711

NEW MEXICO

ROUTE 66 ON TOUR

LEGENDARY ARCHITECTURE

FROM GLENRIO TO

GALLUP

By
Don J. Usner

Photo Editing

by

Louise Stiver

Museum of New Mexico Press
Santa Fe

in collaboration with

New Mexico Historic
Preservation Division

FRONTIS PHOTOGRAPH:
Nine Mile Hill west of
Albuquerque, 1954.

NSET PHOTOGRAPHS:
Top right: Tewa Lodge,
Albuquerque.
Top left: Santo Domingo
Trading Post.
Middle: El Morro
Theatre, Gallup.
Bottom: Lake City Diner,
Santa Rosa.

COVER PHOTOGRAPHS:
Front Cover: Route 66
Diner, Albuquerque.
Photograph by Elmo Baca.
Back Cover: Route 66
through Tijeras Canyon.

Copyright © 2001
New Mexico Historic Preservation Division,
Office of Cultural Affairs.

All rights reserved. No part of this book may be reproduced in any form, with the
exception of brief passages embodied in critical reviews, without the express written
consent of the publisher.

Project editor: Mary Wachs
Design and production: Bruce Taylor Hamilton
Maps: Jan Underwood, Information Illustrated
Composition: Set in Syntax with Insignia display
Manufactured in the United States of America
10 9 8 7 6 5 4 3 2 1

Library of Congress Control Number: 2001 132120
ISBN: 0-89013-386-7

Museum of New Mexico Press
Post Office Box 2087
Santa Fe, New Mexico 87504

This publication has been financed in part with federal funds from the National Park
Service, U.S. Department of the Interior. However, the contents and opinions do not
necessarily reflect the views or policies of the Historic Preservation Division or the
Department of the Interior.

This program received Federal financial assistance for identification and protection of
historic properties. Under Title VI of the Civil Rights Act of 1964, Section 504 of the
Rehabilitation Act of 1973, and the Age Discrimination Act of 1975, as amended, the
U.S. Department of the Interior prohibits discrimination on the basis of race, color,
national origin, disability or age in its federally assisted programs. If you believe you
have been discriminated against in any program, activity, or facility as described above,
or if you desire further information, please write to:

Office of Equal Opportunity
National Park Service
1849 C Street, N.W.
Washington, D.C. 20240

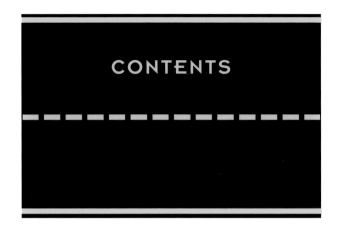

CONTENTS

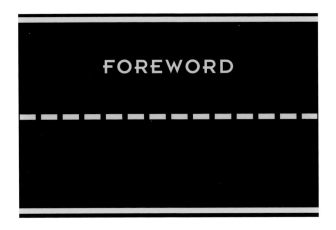

FOREWORD

The year 2001 provides an extraordinary opportunity for us to examine and reflect on the architectural legacy of historic Route 66 in New Mexico. As Albuquerque and other Route 66 communities in the state prepare to welcome thousands of travelers and visitors to celebrate the 75th anniversary of the fabled highway, the New Mexico Historic Preservation Division and Museum of New Mexico Press offer this tribute to the remarkable landmark buildings on Route 66.

Author Don Usner provides a unique and entertaining perspective on the state's Route 66 landmarks. Trained as a cultural geographer, Usner's contribution is to place these distinctive twentieth-century buildings with the time and space and cultural matrix that is New Mexico.

Usner clearly and convincingly asserts that New Mexico presented an exotic and nearly foreign travel experience to early motorists on Route 66. Not only did the landscape transform dramatically as the miles flew by, from the flat expanses of the eastern *llano* to the scenic red bluffs of Gallup, but place names and historical scars on the land also spoke with Castilian, Pueblo, or Navajo accents.

Usner's lively text reminds us to slow down and experience the buildings and landscapes of a great transportation corridor and to reflect on the importance of preserving cultural corridors and architectural sites. Usner's sharp focus reaches beyond buildings and landforms to people, illuminating their peculiar and often surprising reasons for settling and surviving in a given place.

New Mexico Route 66 on Tour serves as a travelogue and also as an overview of the state's best Route 66 roadside architecture. It offers a visual record of some surviving landmarks, preserved with much care and love by their owners and communities, and others which, nearly lost to time and memory, proved nearly as ephemeral as the passing traffic.

With its strategic location roughly midway along the highway between Chicago and Los Angeles, New Mexico offered motorists much more than unusual landscapes and exotic cultures. From its earliest beginnings, Route 66 architecture in New Mexico fused the aspirations of a new American state with the proud design traditions of the ancient Southwest.

In several towns in New Mexico, the course of the great highway closely paralleled the railroad tracks laid down several decades before. Railroad stations and associated buildings thus provided a framework of reference and context for the new buildings catering to motorists.

The Mission Revival style, which engineered for concrete and brick designs born of adobe, became the first southwestern architectural style to gain national favor after 1890. It quickly became a favorite architectural vocabulary for the Atchison, Topeka, and Santa Fe Railway and other lines that crisscrossed New Mexico a century ago.

The most outstanding and beloved monument of the Mission Revival style in the state was surely downtown Albuquerque's Alvarado Hotel, built circa 1902 just a block or two north of the future path of Route 66 along Central Avenue. The gracious Alvarado came to symbolize not only the romantic appeal of Hispanic–Moorish building traditions but also New Mexico's newly developing hospitality industry as well.

Beneath the picturesque arcades and breezeways of the Alvarado, railroad passengers and automobile tourists alike delighted in purchasing Pueblo and Navajo arts and crafts—pottery and weavings—directly from Native Americans. The marketing of Indian arts and crafts proved to be a lucrative attraction on Route 66, influencing a unique type of business and storefront, the curio shop.

Every town and nearly every roadside business offered handmade Indian products for sale. It is still a trademark of touring Route 66 in New Mexico. "Indian" style came to embody much more than arts and crafts, however. By 1920, "modern" Pueblo architectural forms had won favor in the capital city of Santa Fe. Within just a few years, the Pueblo Revival style of architecture had spread like wildfire to major communities, especially to those that were anticipating or enjoying the commerce of Route 66.

Timeless masterpieces were built in the Pueblo Revival fashion in short order soon after Route 66 arrived in 1926. These legendary buildings form the heart of Route 66 landmarks in the state: the Pueblo "Deco" KiMo Theatre in Albuquerque (1927); the Mission and Pueblo Revival hybrid El Navajo Hotel in Gallup (1923–1958); the Franciscan Hotel of Albuquerque (demolished about 1972); the McKinley County Courthouse in Gallup (1938); and the El Vado Motel in Albuquerque (1937).

A new alignment of Route 66 in New Mexico was completed in 1937, bypassing Santa Fe, Bernalillo, Isleta, and Los Lunas and ushering in a faster, more efficient highway experience. Picturesque motor courts and tourist camps in time gave way to family-run "western" motels and later to efficient but standardized franchise operations such as Ramada and Holiday inns. Today's Route

66 adventurers can enjoy nearly the entire architectural spectrum of roadside lodgings. Classic buildings such as Tucumcari's Blue Swallow Motel, Albuquerque's La Posada (formerly the Hilton), and Gallup's El Rancho still welcome weary travelers to spend the night.

Automotive service stations and dealerships have also evolved from homespun businesses to major corporate interests. Simple shed-like garages offering to fix flats for five cents soon competed with the quaint cottages of Phillips 66 and later the sanitary white-and-yellow boxes of the Whiting Brothers. Built nearly a decade ago, the behemoth scale of Giant Travel Center twenty miles east of Gallup signaled a symbolic end to an era when motorists could look forward to real service.

After a hiatus in long-distance motoring during World War II, when gas rationing slowed the flow of cars through the Southwest, Route 66 roared back during the prosperous Cold War years. Young families took advantage of cheap gas, improved superhighways, and legendary high-performance automobiles to explore the wonders of America. Few vacations could rival the Southwest's Route 66 tour in the 1950s and '60s.

Drive-in movie theaters and diners dotted the high desert landscape a few decades ago. Today they are nearly gone. The smilin' fat man of Santa Rosa's Club Café is obscured by golden arches and fading neon.

Looking back in the seventy-five-year legacy of Route 66 in New Mexico, we may take some comfort in how many significant buildings remain along the historic roadside. Some great landmarks have been lost, but enough of the texture and context of New Mexico's Route 66 architecture remains to re-create a memorable motoring experience.

We must admit, however, that some of the magic has been lost. During its heyday, Route 66 not only produced spectacular buildings, it also had a sense of humor. Festive billboards set in sequence (Burma Shave, Club Café Fat Man, Whoa! You Passed It!) told a story and provided amusement at the same time. Roadside tourist traps featuring live buffalo, rattlesnakes, or fake dinosaurs proved irresistible to the naive, young-at-heart, or just plain foolhardy. Other buildings in the form of tepees, forts, or icebergs lent a surreal veneer to the piñon-clad mesas.

Above all, this book is designed to inspire one or more pilgrimages to historic Route 66 in New Mexico. Though the reader can travel down the highway vicariously through these pages, it is the belief of the author, publisher, and the Historic Preservation Division that an actual automobile trip along the Mother Road will prove much more rewarding.

Elmo Baca
New Mexico
Historic Preservation Officer

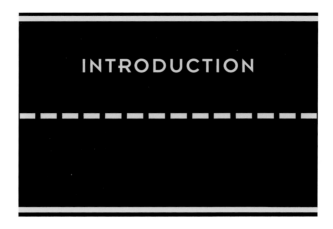

INTRODUCTION

Travelers on Route 66 encountered more diversity in the land and people in New Mexico than in any other segment of the route. Here, perhaps more than in any other state, they were tempted to stray away from the roadway to explore communities and the land, both of which had already been highly mythologized in popular books, movies, and in the promotional literature of the Santa Fe Railway and Fred Harvey Company Indian Detours, among others. While the narrow strip of neon-graced buildings along the route was the primary focus of interest in most places between Chicago and Los Angeles, the experience of the broader and deeper context of "greater Route 66" in New Mexico was at least equally compelling. This broader context of the road—including the land as well as historic buildings and communities along the route and their historical background—is the subject of this book.

Architecture assumes a central place in this travel narrative because architecture—and most particularly, vernacular architecture—reflects conditions imposed by the land and also presents the most visible manifestation of culture. Building styles and materials can serve as a window into the cultural geography along the highway, and the chronology of styles also reveals much about the history of places. The narrative in this book, then, progresses from east to west across the state in guidebook fashion, discussing architecture and cultural geography to evoke the historic context of Route 66. Implicit in this treatment is the idea that by venturing along the remaining segments of Route 66 today, it's still possible to savor the beauty of the land and its cultural diversity and to imagine the landscape as early Route 66 travelers would have seen it.

In considering the architecture along the highway, two related aspects compete for attention: the architecture of structures directly related, in form or function, to Route 66, and the architecture of buildings not connected to the highway. Of course Route 66—and its predecessor in bringing visitors to the state, the Santa Fe Railway—had a profound impact on the towns along its length, encouraging all of them to market themselves to tourists to some degree. But away from the road a separate architectural tradition evolved in the design of homes, subdivisions, and massive public architecture. The two parallel trends were not mutually exclusive, as a regional architectural style developed partly in response to the tastes of visitors coming on the highway (or earlier, the railroad).

For information regarding Route 66–oriented architecture, I relied heavily on a survey sponsored by the New Mexico Historic Preservation Division of the historic and architectural resources of Route 66 in New Mexico. A three-person team completed the Herculean task of surveying and preparing Historic Building Inventory Forms for 557 properties built before 1960, including tourist courts, cafés, curio shops, trading posts, service stations, and municipal roadside attractions. Additionally, the study identified well-preserved segments of roadway or those that conveyed the feeling of travel on Route 66, including historic bridges associated with the highway. The summary report on the survey, written by David Kammer, elaborates an historic framework on the rise of automobile tourism in New Mexico and relates the historical properties to that context.

To expand the narrative beyond the edges of Route 66, I turned to many other sources (see Suggested Reading). The files at the Historic Preservation Division proved invaluable in providing written descriptions of important properties and, in some cases, entire historic communities. I also made a personal reconnaissance of the places described here and filled in detail from my own experience as much as possible. The majority of the historic structures along the route face some level of threat to their integrity, and I found that even the descriptions put down by Kammer's crew in the early 1990s sometimes no longer applied, as buildings were either gone or greatly altered. I hope this presentation will kindle interest in the care and preservation of what remains of Route 66 architecture.

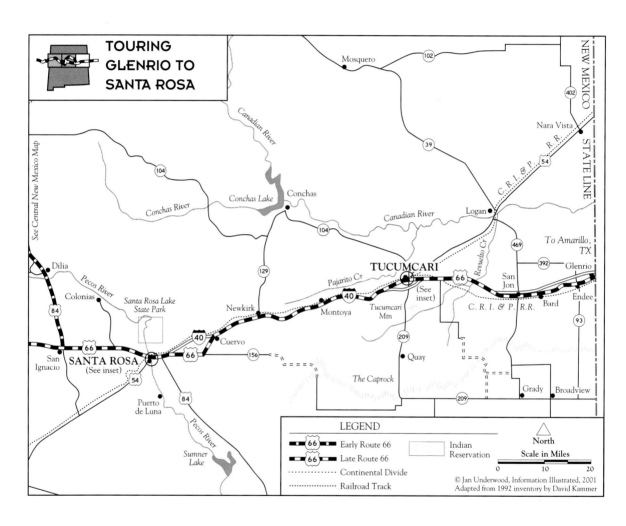

TOURING GLENRIO TO SANTA ROSA

Mosquero

Canadian River

NEW MEXICO STATE LINE

Nara Vista

C. R. I. & P. R. R.

Conchas Lake   Conchas

Conchas River

Canadian River

Logan

Retuelto Cr

To Amarillo, TX

See Central New Mexico Map

Dilia

Pecos River

Colonias

Santa Rosa Lake State Park

TUCUMCARI
(See inset)

Newkirk

Montoya

Tucumcari Mtn

San Jon

Glenrio

Bard

Endee

C. R. I. & P. R. R.

Pajarito Cr

San Ignacio

SANTA ROSA
(See inset)

Cuervo

Quay

The Caprock

Puerto de Luna

Grady   Broadview

Sumner Lake

Pecos River

LEGEND

66 Early Route 66

66 Late Route 66

.... Continental Divide

.... Railroad Track

Indian Reservation

North

Scale in Miles
0   10   20

© Jan Underwood, Information Illustrated, 2001
Adapted from 1992 inventory by David Kammer

TOUR ONE

TOURING GLENRIO
TO
SANTA ROSA

**GLENRIO
TO SAN JON:
WIDE-OPEN
SPACES**

Route 66 followed rail lines into New Mexico across the open expanses of the southern Great Plains and stayed alongside the tracks, for the most part, from Glenrio all the way to Santa Rosa. Beginning at the border at the highway's lowest elevation in New Mexico (3,800 feet above sea level), it ran from railroad town to railroad town, along some of the longest stretches of lonely two-lane blacktop in New Mexico. Some today might call the landscape monotonous, and its dimensions must have been all the more overwhelming when traveled on a two-lane road, which was unpaved for the first several years of the highway's existence. Few pieces of old Route 66 in New Mexico retain the old west feeling of wide-open spaces, and none so starkly as these fragments on New Mexico's Great Plains, where it's still possible to experience unbroken terrain punctuated only by the long ribbon of highway.

From a geographical standpoint, the initial New Mexico stretch of Route 66 belongs to West Texas. Here the ranching culture of the plains retains a dominance it has held since Texas cattlemen pushed north through eastern New Mexico in the late 1800s. But by the time the road reaches Santa Rosa, evidence of New Mexico's Hispanic and Pueblo cultures begins to filter into the landscape. The air begins to feel drier, the land more varied in topographic relief, and juniper trees take root where, to the east, grasses stretch to the horizon. Culturally, a shift becomes clear at Santa Rosa also, as the cowboy culture of the *llano* collides with the farming culture of the Pecos River Valley, a clash vividly fictionalized in Rudolfo Anaya's *Bless Me, Ultima*, one of the most popular novels ever written about New Mexico.

Between Glenrio and San Jon, Route 66 today recreates most fully what early travel on the road would have been like: rugged gravel surface and creosote-treated timber bridges

The name of the first town inside the New Mexico border expresses this meeting of cultures and landscapes: Glenrio, derived from an English word meaning hollow or valley, and a Spanish word meaning river. Never mind that no river or valley exists in the area to explain the name. It suffices to signal that a transition has begun. Unlike the towns farther west in the Rio Grande Valley, whose roots reach deep into the past, there was no predecessor for Glenrio, no Spanish Colonial village foundations for the more modern towns. This far east on Route 66, the towns owe their existence entirely to the railroad, and Glenrio is no exception. It began when the railroad tracks were laid down across the plains in 1902.

The State Line Bar, the Little Juarez Diner, and the First in Texas/Last in Texas Motel and Café drew a lively clientele from passersby on the highway. Now all that remains are the empty whitewashed buildings that once housed a tourist court, a café and a gas station, all of which manifest the Southwest Vernacular style that dominated roadside attractions with increasing frequency westward. The vast majority of the motels along the highway in New Mexico utilized this style, characterized by flat roofs (or shed roofs disguised by irregular parapets), stuccoed walls white or in earth tones, and, sometimes, by window hoods with tile accents.

West of Glenrio, the interlude of bright lights and hot meals ended abruptly, as the land swallowed up the road again. For most of the fifteen miles from **Glenrio to San Jon,** the road's pavement has deteriorated. Its rugged gravel surface thus re-creates what the earliest Route 66 experience must have been like. The dusty track leaves the interstate far behind as it swings to the south, reaching an isolated cluster of buildings in about four miles at Endee, named after the "ND" brand of a nearby ranch. (The town of Bard down the road owes its name to the Bar D brand.) A 1917 travelers' logbook for the road through Endee, printed before Route 66 was designated, announces that "phone, water, stores, [and a] post office" were available at Endee. These services expanded as their clientele increased with Route 66's designation, as evinced by an abandoned four-unit tourist court and gas station by the roadside. Other buildings at Endee comprise the remains of the Endee community, which consisted of houses whose walls were made of vertical poles and roofs covered with sod cut from the grasslands—a kind of construction well suited to the open, nearly treeless plains.

Bridges between Glenrio and Endee date from the 1920s and stand among few survivors of the creosote-treated timber bridges along Route 66. Broken pieces of asphalt cling to their surfaces, which at twenty-four-feet wide seem exceedingly narrow by today's standards. Vintage chain-link guardrails from the 1920s remain on some. The bridges were necessary because, although the plains may be imagined as flat-as-a-pancake terrain, here in the upper Canadian River drainage they are punctuated with dry creek-bed washes. In fact, the parts of Route 66 that cut through this area presented plenty of road-building challenges. The washes, prone to violent flooding during summer thunderstorms, posed one problem. Equally daunting was the lack of suitable local aggregate for surfacing the road. The natural substrate of sand and caliche (salt-impregnated clay) became extremely slippery when saturated and produced dust in prodigious quantities when dry.

About ten miles west of Endee, old Route 66 swings back to Interstate 40 at San Jon. Pronounced as if it were a Spanish name ("San Hone") by locals, the

"Greetings
from Tucumcari,"
postcard by J. R. Willis,
ca. 1951

Route 66
through Tucumcari.
Photograph by C. E. Redman,
ca. 1945.

name has no meaning in Spanish, although a likely origin for the word is *zanjón*, which means "deep gully" and may refer to nearby San Jon creek. The town sprang up as a shipping point along a siding when the railroad came through in 1902 and grew with the designation of Route 66. Photos from the 1930s show a small roadside strip at San Jon, including a port of entry station. San Jon still draws travelers as an active service center for Interstate 40 traffic, with new, large gas stations along the new road and abandoned Route 66 businesses astride the old road a few blocks to the south.

Interstate 40 and old Route 66 coincide for most of the distance from San Jon to Tucumcari. Here Route 66 engineers faced new road building and maintenance challenges. In addition to the major washes of Revuelto and Plaza Larga Creeks, where summer floods washed out bridge approaches repeatedly, a natural lake just east of Tucumcari often over-flowed and inundated the roadway during the rainy season. Lacking a raised gravel bed, the road would remain waterlogged for days, forcing highway officials to send out teams of horses to pull automobiles through the muck. An alternative was to build long corduroys of railroad ties across the quagmire.

TUCUMCARI
TONIGHT!

The lake by Tucumcari, situated near a major east-west trade corridor following the Canadian River Valley, had been an important watering place for many years before the town existed. Bands of Comanches rested and watered their horses here, as did *comancheros*, as Hispanic traders from the Rio Grande Valley were called. When Goodnight and Loving blazed their famous cattle-driving trail through they also stopped at the lake. The town's name probably comes from the Comanche word for a promontory, now called Tucumcari Mountain, which rises to 5,000-feet elevation just southeast of Tucumcari. Written mention of the locale goes back to 1777, but there is no evidence of a town at the site until the Chicago, Rock Island, and Pacific Railroad laid tracks through in 1902. The tent city at the siding went by "Rag Town" and "Six Shooter Siding" before its first formal designation as Douglas and, later, Tucumcari. The town grew rapidly when the railroad located repair shops there.

TUCUMCARI'S
MOTEL MILE

By the 1930s automobile traffic eclipsed railroad passenger travel in New Mexico. The railroads began to decline, but Tucumcari was able to survive due to its location on the newly designated Route 66. The town presented travelers on Route 66 with their first major motel strip in New Mexico, well announced for many miles by billboards bearing the slogan "Tucumcari Tonight!" The motels along the strip in Tucumcari boasted names that would appeal to travelers' sense of adventure, many of which remain: the Pony Soldier, the Lasso, the Palomino, and the Cactus RV

Built by local carpenter W. A. Huggins between 1939 and 1941, the Blue Swallow Motel has retained its Southwest Vernacular elements and is one of the best examples of a pre–World War II tourist court remaining along Route 66 in New Mexico. The motel's showy neon sign, which dates to the late 1950s, catches the driver's attention with the figure of a flashing blue swallow. Photographed in 1991.

Park call to mind images of cowboys and the ranching west, while the Kiva RV Park and the Apache Motel (as well as the tepee-shaped **TeePee Curio Shop**) exploit romantic notions of the region's Indian heritage. Here in Tucumcari the Royal Palacio alone reflects the Spanish and Mexican history of the region. Towns westward increasingly offer the flavor of this history.

In architectural style, most of these motels express western themes to varying degrees. The Redwood Lodge, constructed to resemble a rambling ranch house, offers a good example. Several other motels on the strip possess at least modest stylistic details of the Southwest Vernacular style. References to this regional style may be conveyed with just a slight parapet on a pitched roof, while at others the suggestion is stronger. The brown stucco, rounded corners and a well-articulated parapet on the Cactus RV Park, for example (once an L-shaped court built of stone), give it a pronounced "southwestern" look.

The **Blue Swallow** has kept its form since the 1930s, interior and exterior, and is one of the best examples of early tourist courts still in existence along Route 66 in New Mexico. The tourist court comprises a single-story room block laid out in an L-shape along with a single-story, free-standing office that at one time served as a gas station. The buildings frame an open space where a playground offered road-sick children respite from miles of travel. Garage units with overhead wooden doors are interspersed with the thirteen sleeping units. Pink stucco and a subtle parapet, highlighted in blue paint and blue neon lighting, give just the slightest allusion to Southwest Vernacular style. The motel's large, showy neon sign rests on the office roof and a freestanding post support, form-

The motels along the strip in Tucumcari were named to appeal to the traveler's sense of adventure in a new landscape, and many of these remain. The Palomino Motel, photographed in 1991, is a good example of classic 1950s motel architecture.

Places such as the Tee Pee exploit romantic notions of New Mexico's Indian heritage. This curio shop and former deli and gas station, photographed in 1991, was built by Leland Hayes in Southwest Vernacular style architecture.

ing an arch canopy under which prospective clients can park. The sign, which dates to the 1950s, attracts the eye with the figure of a flashing blue swallow—a motif that is repeated, once again in blue neon, periodically along the facade.

Phares Huggins remembers that his father, W. A. Huggins, built the Blue Swallow between 1939 and 1941, using stout hollow-tile bricks for the walls. A local plasterer added a bit of flair to the finish by troweling in fan-like impressions and using two colors of plaster. The colorful stucco was one of the most striking features of the motel. Unfortunately, Huggins was forced to sell the Blue Swallow almost immediately after it was completed because, as his son remembers it, the rationing of fuel and materials that began with the onset of World War II depleted Route 66 of travelers. Lillian Redman bought it and managed it for forty years, but subsequent owners made alterations that diminished the motel's historic character. The current proprietors have done painstaking restoration.

DOWN ALONG THE TRACKS: DOWNTOWN TUCUMCARI

Reflecting Tucumcari's origins as a railroad town, the oldest business district is oriented toward the railway station a few blocks north of the more modern commercial strip. In most railroad towns, railroad developers platted towns along the route and profited from selling real estate when the tracks were laid. In Tucumcari, however, a group of businessmen anticipated the building boom that would accompany the arrival of the rails and incorporated the Tucumcari Townsite and Investment Company in 1901 to develop a townsite. The Chicago, Rock Island, and Pacific (CRI&P) Railroad entered town from the northeast the following year, and the main commercial street was laid out perpendicular to the rail lines. A residential grid spread from this nucleus.

Before long, Tucumcari had three more railroads and thrived in its role as a maintenance center: in 1902 the El Paso and Southwestern Railroad Company connected Tucumcari to El Paso on the Golden State Route that ran from Chicago to Southern California; the El Paso and Northwestern Railroad System laid tracks into Tucumcari from the north in 1903; and the CRI&P added a line to the east of town in 1910 and in 1924, Tucumcari became the division point between the Southern Pacific and CRI&P, where crews and equipment changed and passengers stopped for meals.

At the center of the web of rail lines, where First Street and Railroad Avenue meet, the CRI&P built the local **Tucumcari train depot** in 1926. The new rail station became a focus of community life. The depot, although no longer in use, is the last remaining railroad building from the town's pre-1930 era that has not been altered beyond recognition.

The depot is made of brick laid in the Mission Revival style, which evolved in Southern California in the late nineteenth century as architects sought to define a historic style based on regional Spanish Colonial prototypes. The Mission Revival style, with its wide overhangs and open arches, was particularly well suited to train stations in the warm, dry, southwestern climate. The Southern Pacific and the Atchison, Topeka and Santa Fe (AT&SF) railways used the style in the first decades of the twentieth century for elaborate depots in major cities. In New Mexico, however, the Southern Pacific employed older wooden structures, while the AT&SF introduced the Mission Revival style to New Mexico. The AT&SF built or remodeled most of its New Mexico depots in the Mission Revival style. Later, the railroad used the Pueblo Revival style—a style that became very popular among motel builders, second in popularity to the Southwest Vernacular Style. The regional revival styles became something of a trademark for the line.

The CRI&P line was not well known for using the Mission Revival style, but it, too, sought to capture in depot architecture the romantic, historical associations of the ultimate destination of its western routes in California. Tucumcari was effectively the western terminus of the CRI&P, and the company elected to build one of the most fully developed examples of the style here. The Tucumcari depot contrasted with the one at Liberal, Kansas, which took the same general form but was smaller and incorporated less elaborate Mission Revival detailing. Though modest in size, the Tucumcari depot included, under

The Chicago, Rock Island, and Pacific (CRI&P) train depot was built in 1926 in Mission Revival style and included a restaurant, waiting room, ticket windows, express freight and mailroom, and offices. Fashioned as one long building, the structure's most striking feature is its bold, curvilinear parapets, which front both ends of the building as well as each cross gable.

The architectural firm of Townes and Funk chose the Art Deco style when designing the Quay County Courthouse. Built in 1939 with Works Progress Administration funding, it resembles other New Deal courthouses in the Southwest.

one roof, a restaurant, waiting room, ticket windows, express freight and mailroom, and offices.

The Tucumcari station is a long, narrow one-story building, stuccoed creamy white above the lower edge of the windows and boasting a red-tiled gable roof. The building's most striking feature is its bold, curvilinear parapets, which front both ends of the building as well as each cross gable. The cross gables intersect the length of the building twice, at about the middle and near the west end. Small, one-story projections, decorated by curvilinear parapets like those above, extend from all but one of the cross gables. At each end of the building a slight projection fronts the parapet with lines echoing those on the side projections. Most of the depot's windows and doorways are arched.

After World War II, Tucumcari's position as a railroad town declined with the widespread adoption of diesel engines and the popularity of the new national highway system. The machine shops, roundhouse, and other facilities in Tucumcari dedicated to steam engines closed and were eventually torn down. Passenger and eventually freight service ended on the Tucumcari-to-Memphis route. Passenger service through Tucumcari on the Golden State Route came to an end in 1968. The former train depot, the sole remaining railroad building, now serves as a rail yard office.

As Route 66 rose in importance, Tucumcari's business district shifted south toward the new highway. Downtown's old business and associated residential neighborhoods remain in good condition, however, and provide clear examples of the architecture from the 1930s through the 1950s. A few buildings of Pueblo Revival style, with their simulated adobe finishes and modest portals, are tucked among houses of diverse styles typical of the Midwest and West Texas. The southwestern regional styles stand out as anomalies here in Tucumcari, whereas by the time the highway reaches Santa Fe, the trends are reversed.

The **Quay County Courthouse** occupies a block on Third Street in the old residential area. In the Rio Grande Valley, architects designing a courthouse in the 1930s would have been tempted to use a Pueblo Revival or other regional design. In Santa Fe, they would practically have been required to do so. The architectural firm Townes and Funk elected instead to use Art Deco style in Quay County's new courthouse, a more contemporary, nationally popular style that the firm had employed for the more ambitious Colfax County Courthouse in Raton. The courthouse resembles public buildings of West Texas, again confirming the ties of this part of New Mexico with its neighbors to the east.

The courthouse, built in 1939 and supported by Works Progress Administration funding, is situated in a Shelbyville courthouse square plan (a kind of arrangement first established in Shelbyville, Kentucky, and imitated across the South). Built of concrete, cast stone, and granite, the structure has a flat roof with a cast stone parapet and consists of stepped massing with a four-story center mass. The building displays a heavy massing with a marble base area and concrete foundation but the aluminum casement windows, recessed into the bays (or vertical divisions) to enhance the building's verticality. Two broad, low flights of stairs, flanked by the telescoping wings, lead to the main entrance on the northeast facade. Cast concrete bas-reliefs of ranchers and railroad laborers at work decorate the middle wings, celebrating the major industries of the region at the time the courthouse was built. Cast stone cow heads top pilasters on the front facade, reemphasizing the ranching history of the town.

Terrazzo floors, plaster ceilings, and marble walls in the lobby area detail the interior of the courthouse. Other details include Deco-style light fixtures, handrails, and grilles and aluminum bas-relief justice symbols embellishing the second-floor courtroom. One of the most unusual features of the interior décor is a large mural above the courtroom door. Created by Ben Carlton Mead in 1939, the mural depicts the Spanish explorer, Francisco Vásquez de Coronado, and his entourage crossing the plains near Tucumcari, accompanied by cross-bearing, brown-robed friars who are ministering to Native Americans. Beneath the image an inscription reads: "I came this way and left my mark." This

The Westerner Drive-Inn, opened in the mid-1950s, was a favorite for Route 66 travelers. This Southwest Vernacular style drive-in, photographed in 1992, recently closed.

acknowledgment of the Spanish Colonial imprint on the Southwest seems somewhat odd, as evidence that Coronado traveled through the area is anecdotal and the Spanish Colonial presence in the region was negligible. But like the hints of Pueblo Revival styling on buildings, the Coronado mural anticipates an increasing fascination westward with all things "Spanish."

DUSTY RAILROAD TOWNS ON THE PLAINS: PALOMAS TO CUERVO

In the 1930s, Route 66 businesses tapered west of Tucumcari's downtown core as the road began another trek across wide-open country. Between Tucumcari and Santa Rosa, two segments of the route have not been significantly altered since the 1930s. The first, a 10-mile section of frontage road between Palomas and Montoya, stays close to the interstate for most of its length, passing through the Pajarito Creek Valley with Mesa Rica to the north and Palomas Mesa to the south. The landscape elements, the nearby railroad grade, and the low telephone line paralleling the road all contribute to a strong feeling of travel across rural New Mexico in the early twentieth century. Three bridges located between six and eight miles from Palomas are noteworthy for their historic context and design. Built in 1933 with Works Progress Administration (WPA) funding, each single-span bridge measures approximately forty feet in length and is made of reinforced concrete beams with concrete abutments. Concrete curbs and reinforced concrete railings flank their twenty-four-foot-wide concrete decks, and WPA project numbers are affixed to their concrete end posts.

As the road approaches Montoya—a town that started as a shipping point on the CRI&P railroad—it diverges from its close parallel with Interstate 40, passing a series of small roadside businesses, vacant and deteriorating, as well as the Montoya cemetery. Montoya is a venerable family name in New Mexico that was applied to this area when New Mexico's governor granted some 655,000 acres to Pablo Montoya. The Montoya Grant and the overlapping Baca Location Number 2 Grant were the easternmost of the land grants made in New Mexico under Spanish and later Mexican rule and as such represent another marker of the edges of the deep-rooted Hispanic homeland. From this point westward, land grants originally established individual and community ownership of land—ownership that American settlers challenged and in many cases wrested from the rightful New Mexican heirs.

G.W. Richardson established the first incarnation of the **Richardson's Store** in 1908 at the original townsite of Montoya, north of the railroad tracks, when homesteaders were moving in and claiming land in the area. The farming boom quickly collapsed due to the fickle rainfall of New Mexico's eastern plains, and the store saw fewer and fewer patrons from the dwindling farming community.

Fortunately for the enterprise, at about the same time that farming declined and was replaced by more dispersed ranching operations, federal funds became available for constructing Route 66. The family moved the store across the tracks to its present location to take advantage of traffic on the newly designated highway. After previously serving as a mercantile store for ranchers, farmers, and local railroad workers, the store adapted to serve travelers on the highway.

The Richardson's Store is now closed up and fenced off from access, but as late as the 1980s it offered a shady refuge to travelers on Route 66 and Interstate 40 and still offers an excellent example of an early twentieth-century general store. The L-shaped, hip-roofed structure is built of local red sandstone scavenged from buildings in the village of Montoya across the tracks, which is largely abandoned except for the sprawling buildings and corrals of the T4 Ranch headquarters. The store's 1930s-era facade is composed of two plate-glass show windows on each side of the wood-

In typical curio-shop fashion, the windows of Richardson's Store in Montoya once displayed locally gathered geological specimens, arrowheads, vintage barbed wire, and rattlesnake rattles. Richardson's served locals and travelers alike into the 1980s.
Interior of store photograph by Richard Federici, 1977.

framed glass doors of the store's entrance. In typical curio-shop fashion, the windows once displayed locally gathered artifacts—including geological specimens, arrowheads, bits of old barbed wire, and a collection of rattlesnake rattles—in addition to groceries and picnic supplies.

A tall flagpole stands alongside a garish Gulf Oil sign in front of the store, and a small wooden sign at ground level identifies the building as the U.S. Post Office. A heavy portico, painted white, extends forward to cover two gasoline pumps and to protect the store's front entrance. The building's west wall is also painted white and bears the legend "Richardson Store" stenciled in large black letters. The Richardson residence extends across the whole south end of the structure. Additions to the building include a small, wooden pump house topped by a shed roof at the building's northeast corner and a small addition to the living space. East of the building, sheltered from the incessant west winds, a small garden comprised of native plants and shaded by tall elms used to be a favorite picnic spot for visitors.

Heading west from Montoya, old Route 66 is accessible only in short sections. The old railroad/Route 66 town of Newkirk contains a few abandoned roadside businesses—including a tiny, four-unit tourist court—and a chapel that looks intriguingly similar to the small churches in the Pecos and Rio Grande valleys, but the next best place along the route to exit the freeway and drive the old highway comes at **Cuervo**. A post office and a few modern, highway-related businesses are still in operation at Cuervo along a tiny commercial strip. Businesses that served the old highway stand alongside new ones, including an abandoned Texaco station made out of a railroad car, with its sign still intact. Beside a wooden structure with a portal stands a deserted grocery store made of adobe. The residential part of town spreads out on both sides of the railroad tracks and old Route 66, down the sloping plain toward Cuervo Creek and up to the base of a low sandstone mesa. The architecture of this ghost town gives a flavor of much older towns farther west in New Mexico, although Cuervo can only trace its roots to 1901 or 1902. There are many broken-down and deteriorating buildings of adobe and of sandstone, most with pitched roofs. Amid the vacant houses, Cuervo's graceful stone church is well maintained and bears an inscription of its date of construction, 1915, and its builder, Max Salas. The very presence of the chapels here and at Newkirk announces the increasing presence of a devout, Hispanic Catholic populace and mirrors the demographic trend away from the Protestant-dominated towns to the east.

From Cuervo, Route 66 turns to the southwest, making an unusual break away from the railroad tracks and embarking on a seven-mile diversion—marked as abandoned on some maps—that can still be driven to its junction with unpaved State Road 156, which heads arrow-straight to Santa Rosa. Some concrete culverts, a faded yellow center stripe, and modest cut banks remain along the old road as it climbs slowly up Sunshine Mesa, but the wide-open expanse of the landscape surrounding the narrow road—heightened by the absence of the railroad or other structures—gives a strong sense of what travel was like here before the interstate highway was built. Ruins of an old adobe homestead with a broken-down windmill nearby remind us that the route wasn't always devoid of humanity. The road drops to cross a deep arroyo on Cuervito Creek, then climbs two hundred vertical feet to the top of Mesa Contadero, where a gas station awaited Route 66 motorists. All that remains are the foundations and concrete pump island.

SANTA ROSA: A GEM ON THE PECOS

State Road 156 obliterated traces of Route 66 but the newer road still offers scenic vistas that would have impressed travelers on the old road as they approached **Santa Rosa**, situated above the floodplain of the Pecos River. The shallow valley of the Pecos is one of New Mexico's two principal agricultural river valleys. Arrival at the Pecos meant intensified contact with the farthest tendrils of the old Hispanic culture of New Mexico. During most of the Spanish Colonial period, Hispanic colonists were confined to the Rio Grande Valley, hemmed in by pressures from nomadic Indian groups on all sides. But by the early nineteenth century, settlers had made the leap over mountain barriers and entered the Pecos River Valley, where they established farming and ranching towns. Settlement spread slowly down the river over the ensuing decades, reaching Puerto de Luna in the 1860s.

State officials declared Puerto de Luna the county seat of Guadalupe County, and it stayed the largest town in the region for decades. Santa Rosa, first called Agua Negra Chiquita, started five years after Puerto de Luna, ten miles upriver. The first postmaster of Santa Rosa, Celso Baca, is credited with renaming the town, perhaps after his wife, Rosa. The small but elegant stone chapel that Baca built and devoted to Santa Rosa de Lima in 1890, now partially in ruins, still stands a few blocks off of old Route 66 on the road to Puerto de Luna.

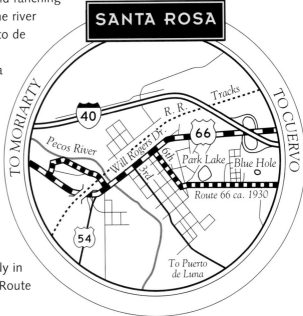

Santa Rosa was just another small farming and ranching town on the Pecos until 1901, when the CRI&P railroad laid tracks through town and it became an important transportation service center. It soon outgrew Puerto de Luna and was named county seat in 1907. Route 66 rejoined the railroad tracks at Santa Rosa and originally came into town by the Blue Hole, a natural spring and deep pool that is the source of Santa Rosa Creek. By the 1930s, the route had shifted north to its present alignment, and over the next two decades a commercial strip developed to serve travelers. Some of the businesses still operate today, and names such as La Mesa Motel, Motel La Loma, Coronado Court, and La Fiesta Drive-In (now Joseph's Restaurant) show an increasing trend toward marketing the region's Hispanic heritage. In the midst of the strip in Santa Rosa, the Route 66 Auto Museum displays vintage autos that recall the models that were popular on the main drag during Route 66's golden years.

**DOWNTOWN
SANTA ROSA**

The heart of old downtown flanks the thoroughfare—here Fourth Street—that begins at the old railroad depot and runs perpendicular to the railroad tracks. The glory days of the railroad are all but forgotten and its importance to Santa Rosa recalled only in the vacant old Ilfeld Warehouse, which lies between Route 66 and the tracks. On the other side of the highway, the small downtown business block hugs the western side of Fourth Street and still conveys a sense of the old town. Santa Rosa is typical in layout and style to many other railroad town commercial districts, although here the buildings are made of local, reddish sandstone instead of the usual brick. On the corner of Fourth and Route 66, the **Lake City Diner** preserves the old architecture best. Built in 1901, it was home to the First National Bank building until 1956. The original tin roof and marble floors remain from the original bank, and the tellers' hardwood cages enjoy new life incorporated into an elegant lunch counter.

The former **Guadalupe County Courthouse** stands across the street from the downtown shops on Fourth. The most impressive architecture in town, the courthouse was built in 1909 of the same reddish sandstone as the other buildings. In style, the courthouse imitates the smaller and less sophisticated courthouse in Puerto de Luna; both were built in the then-popular Richardsonian Romanesque style. The stature of the building has been diminished through

The Guadalupe County Courthouse was built in 1909 in the popular Richardsonian Romanesque style. It has not been attributed to a specific architect but bears an uncanny resemblance to the former Culberson County Courthouse in Van Horn, Texas, which was designed by E. E. Church in 1912.
Photograph by Richard Federici, 1975.

Ilfeld Courthouse.
Photograph by Don Usner, 2001.

neglect and deterioration and because the building now shares its Shelbyville courthouse square plane with the newer (1946) courthouse and still newer jail, neither of which harmonize in style with the historic building.

The Santa Rosa courthouse has not been attributed to a specific architect, but it bears an uncanny resemblance to the former Culberson County Courthouse in Van Horn, Texas, which was designed by E. E. Church in 1912. Some have suggested it may have been Church's "first run" on the design, especially since, perhaps unintentionally, he gave the Santa Rosa courthouse slightly undersized windows and disproportionate parapet. These unusual twists prompted one architect to label the courthouse "a charming local adaptation of a nationally popular style."

The courthouse is a two-story, rectangular building with carved, classical detailing. Pedimented and capped false parapet walls of varying heights top its hipped roof on four sides. Carved sandstone eagle and urns once topped the building's four corners but only one eagle remains. The false parapet on the southwest (front) facade is larger than the others and is embellished with engaged stone pilasters, a central, circular decorative stone inlay, and a cast panel which reads COURTHOUSE, in case there was any doubt. The front facade consists of a central mass and two flanking bays. Its second story is detailed with fluted stone pilasters with eagle motif capitals and a central enlarged window with dark stone quoins and arched transom. Windows on the second floor in the central section are arched, as is the centrally located opening over the main entrance. The entrance arch is framed with slender, carved stone columns.

Although Route 66 was decertified in 1985 and many miles of its alignment have been erased with the construction of Interstate 40 across New Mexico, much evidence of the earlier road remains. These abandoned portions, some maintained as county roads, appear as archaeological remnants, such as this section southwest of Cuervo.

A half-mile from downtown Santa Rosa, old Route 66 crossed the Pecos River and climbed out of the valley and back on to rolling plains, passing the Texaco Service Station (now Chief Auto Parts) on its way out of town. Prior to 1937, the highway turned north seventeen miles from town to recross the Pecos and begin its 180-mile detour to the north. After the road was realigned in 1937, the highway followed a westward course from Santa Rosa along the same alignment that Interstate 40 now follows to Moriarty, where the old route is again accessible. The rerouting shaved 107 miles off of Route 66 in New Mexico.

After leaving the Pecos Valley at Santa Rosa, it climbed steadily for miles to a high point at Clines Corners—a climb of over 2,400 feet—where the high elevation encourages pine trees to grow amid the diminutive piñon and juniper forest. The high vantage also affords views of the Sangre de Cristo Mountains to the north, which represent the trailing edge of the Southern Rocky Mountains. To the west, the mountain barriers that had dissuaded road builders are barely a blip on the horizon.

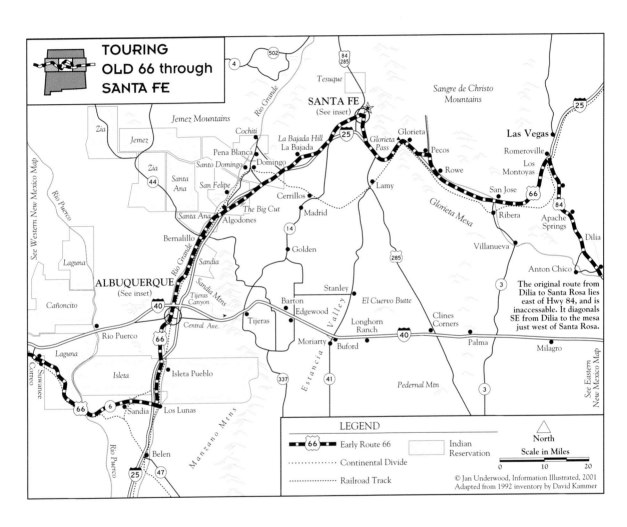

TOURING OLD 66 through SANTA FE

4 · 502

Tesuque

84 · 285

SANTA FE
(See inset)

Sangre de Christo
Mountains

25

Rio Grande

Jemez Mountains

Zia

Jemez

Cochiti

La Bajada Hill
La Bajada

Glorieta
Pass

Glorieta

Pecos

Las Vegas

Romeroville

Los
Montoyas

Pena Blanca

25

Zia

44

Santo Domingo

Domingo

Rowe

San Jose

66

*Santa
Ana*

San Felipe

Cerrillos

Lamy

Glorieta Mesa

Ribera

84

Apache
Springs

Dilia

Santa Ana

Algodones

The Big Cut

Madrid

Villanueva

Bernalillo

14

Sandia

Golden

285

Anton Chico

See Western New Mexico Map

Rio Puerco

Laguna

Rio Grande

3

The original route from
Dilia to Santa Rosa lies
east of Hwy 84, and is
inaccessible. It diagonals
SE from Dilia to the mesa
just west of Santa Rosa.

ALBUQUERQUE
(See inset)

*Sandia
Mtns*

Stanley

El Cuervo Butte

40

Tijeras Canyon

Barton

Clines
Corners

Cañoncito

66

Central Ave.

Tijeras

Edgewood

Longhorn
Ranch

40

Palma

Milagro

Laguna

Isleta

Isleta Pueblo

Moriarty

Buford

Pedernal Mtn

3

*Suwanee
Correo*

66

Rio Puerco

6

Sandia

Los Lunas

337

41

*Estancia
Valley*

Manzano Mtns

Belen

25

47

See Eastern New Mexico Map

LEGEND

━■━ 66 ━■━ Early Route 66

· · · · · · Continental Divide

～～～ Railroad Track

☐ Indian Reservation

△ North

Scale in Miles
0 · · · 10 · · · 20

© Jan Underwood, Information Illustrated, 2001
Adapted from 1992 inventory by David Kammer

TOUR TWO

TOURING OLD 66
THROUGH
SANTA FE

From 1926 until it was rerouted in 1937, Route 66 took a long detour starting west of Santa Rosa. In planning the course of Route 66, planners elected here to deviate from established rail lines, which head southward from Santa Rosa, and to avoid cutting a new road to Moriarty, where other old roads could have been overhauled to bring the highway to Albuquerque. Rather than dealing with the difficult mountain barriers east of Albuquerque, engineers directed Route 66 far to the north, where it rejoined railroad tracks to breach the Rocky Mountains at their southern terminus just east of Santa Fe. From Santa Fe, the road snaked down the Rio Grande Rift Valley through Albuquerque—a diversion through New Mexico's heartland and along its oldest and most well-traveled colonial road, the Camino Real. By the time it continued on a westward course toward California at Los Lunas the road had meandered over 180 miles. It was as if the land was determined to slow travelers' westward progress so that they could dally in this landscape, already widely touted in tourist literature as a place attuned to a slower pace of life.

**HUDDLED FOR
DEFENSE:
PLAZA TOWNS
ON THE PECOS**

As it passed through Spanish Colonial plaza towns and Pueblos made of adobe and stone, the circuitous route exposed travelers headed west to innumerable examples of vernacular architecture they had glimpsed only occasionally in towns farther east. It also bisected downtown Santa Fe just when architects, artists, and city planners were in the midst of reshaping the town's image, creating and advancing new building styles based on the local vernacular. Traveling the old route today still shows both these sources of vernacular style in the rural towns and their carefully planned derivatives in Santa Fe, the adobe capital of the Southwest.

The initial segment of the prealignment route followed relatively gentle tablelands adjacent to the Pecos River Valley northward to Romeroville. Like the larger and more populated Rio Grande Valley to the west, the Pecos Valley has always been a magnet in an arid land. Both rivers arise in the Southern Rocky Mountains but their courses and histories diverge from there. The Rio Grande Valley was home to agricultural communities for centuries before the Spanish arrived, but Pueblo people only lightly occupied the Pecos Valley, whose proximity to the Great Plains proved both a blessing and a liability: the bonus of easy access to bison herds and trading networks on the plains was balanced by the fact that nomadic hunters of the plains sometimes turned to raiding and found easy targets in settled towns.

Spanish colonists faced the same dangers in the Pecos drainage, as had their Pueblo predecessors. For two centuries, the Spanish Colonial occupation of the Pecos Valley was negligible, repeatedly discouraged by hostile attacks. By the eighteenth century, however, Spanish military campaigns had contained the most threatening raiders, the Comanches, and colonists extended a tentative presence into the Pecos Valley. The earliest villages there were settled at the close of the eighteenth century, the twilight of the Spanish Colonial era. As on other parts of New Mexico's Spanish Colonial frontier, the initial forays to settle these towns in the wild Pecos country included a fair proportion of *genízaros*, or ransomed Indians who had been Christianized and lived as Spaniards. Generally considered to be of lower social status, genízaros were capable of communicating with Native tribes and often knew something of the terrain in places outside of Spanish control.

Most Hispanic towns on the upper Pecos conformed to a plaza-type layout and shared characteristic building styles. Because their isolation sheltered them from the impacts experienced by towns in the more populous Rio Grande Valley, their plaza forms are remarkably well preserved. Each originally took the shape of a square or rectangle, its sides formed of adjoined buildings. In some, an additional wall around the town at one time augmented the town's defensive posture. A church was located in a prominent position in the middle of the plazas of all but the smallest towns. Spanish Colonial law mandated that all frontier towns be constructed in this manner to increase their chances of survival in a hostile land and to provide a bulwark against American or French claims on New Mexico.

Houses in the Pecos Valley plazas were built of adobe bricks mortared and plastered with mud, although an abundance of red sandstone prompted some residents to fashion their walls of stone. Interior mud floors were packed and plastered to a smooth surface, sometimes made harder and more durable by admixing ox or cow blood. Standard roof structure consisted of unfinished log beams called *vigas* overlain by small-diameter branches from cedar trees, called *latillas*. A layer of dirt, sometimes a foot or two thick, completed the roof. Water drained from these flat roofs through small wooden ducts known as *canales*. The mud roofs demanded constant maintenance, and virtually all homeowners chose to erect metal roofs, usually pitched or hipped and often with dormers, over the original roofs when the railroad made these materials available in the late nineteenth century.

Adornments on these simple but functional buildings were few. Some houses had *portales* along their long axes, supported by slender posts topped with corbel-like supports called *zapatas*. After Americanization of the region, other stylistic touches were adopted, such as pedimented lintels and squared porch posts. Windows, which were few or totally absent in colonial times, became more common and larger as glass was more available and cheaper, and wooden floors became the norm. Other than these superficial changes, however, the architecture of the small plaza towns has changed little. Pecos Valley buildings don't attempt to make a design statement but instead reflect the exigencies and opportunities of living in this place.

All the basic elements of building design in these villages—and the associated Spanish jargon—from adobe construction to vigas to flat roofs, found their way into the sophisticated and carefully contrived buildings constructed in Santa Fe in the early twentieth century. Back then the conceivers of "Santa Fe style" didn't need to look as far as the Pecos Valley for examples of the vernacular architecture on which to base their plans. The town of Santa Fe still contained numerous old, flat-roofed adobes, designed and built by their owners. The Santa Fe clique leading the charge toward a remake of the city systematically searched out interesting architectural details, however, and their quest sometimes took them as far afield as the Pecos country.

Located halfway between Santa Rosa and Romeroville, the town of Dilia offered Route 66 travelers a good spot for rest and refueling. The former general store/post office is a good example of Southwest Vernacular style.
Photograph by Don Usner, 2001.

DALLYING
IN
DILIA

Highway travelers coming up the valley in the 1920s and '30s were moving in the direction opposite to that taken by Hispanics moving into the valley a century before. Route 66 didn't go directly through the main plaza towns of the Pecos Valley, but just twenty-six miles after turning northward from its east-west corridor, the route crossed the Pecos River and came to **Dilia**. It's difficult to make out the outlines of a plaza at Dilia, and one may not have ever existed there, but a stone church stands at the center of the collection of homes comprised by the modern town. Local people recall that the town used to be called El Vado de Juan Paiz until around the turn of the twentieth century, when it took the name of the local postmaster, Delia Casaus. The post office, general store, and bus station, they say, were all housed in a grand old, two-story structure made of stone that still stands behind the church. The size and design of the building suggest it belongs to a more modern era than the humbler homes in Dilia. The town is located about halfway between Santa Rosa and Romeroville, and it offered Route 66 travelers a good spot for refueling or spending the night. A two-story hotel built of local stone once stood a few hundred feet east of the highway, but its walls are crumbling and the roof has caved in. Immediately fronting the highway, the remnants of a service station and grocery that served Route 66 customers still stand; the building's whitewashed walls and curved, adobe-like lines reflect the typical Southwest Vernacular style of Route 66 businesses.

Other than its passage through Dilia, Route 66 passed close by structures built in the vernacular style only occasionally, as in the vicinity of Los Montoyas and Apache Springs, some seventeen miles north of Dilia, where fine examples of the old stone and adobe buildings remain along the route. It was only a short side trip for a Route 66 traveler to enter plaza towns near the highway, however. Only five miles from Dilia, the river town of Anton Chico, founded in 1822, preserves many old buildings and traces of the old plaza. Colonias de San José and Placita de Abajo, which budded from Anton Chico in the 1860s and 1880s respectively, lie downriver.

CROSSING THE PECOS AND LEAVING THE PLAINS: SAN MIGUEL DEL VADO

The closest plazas to the route are also the two oldest in the valley, **San Miguel del Vado** and San José. San Miguel del Vado was the most important trade town and the jumping-off point for settlement of the Pecos country, as villages spread from there up and down the Pecos Valley in the 1800s. About a dozen of those who petitioned for the San Miguel del Vado land grant on the Pecos River in 1794 were genízaros. Among them were Comanches whose relationships with their nomadic kin may have helped the town to survive. A few hangers-on from Pecos Pueblo joined the land grant claimants, adding to the ethnic diversity of this frontier outpost.

San Miguel del Vado was a vital trade center during the settlement of the Pecos Valley in the 1800s. The Spanish Colonial church of San Miguel del Vado, built in 1811, dominates the surrounding landscape.

San Miguel del Vado is situated at the ford, or *vado*, where a major trail from the plains crossed the Pecos River. When the Santa Fe Trail opened in 1821, the plaza town prospered as the port of entry to New Mexico, and it remained the largest and most important town on the upper Pecos until being gradually eclipsed by Las Vegas beginning in the 1840s. The shape of its old plaza is still discernible as two large, half plazas, although many of its buildings are in ruins. Blocks of houses surround the east half of the old plaza, while the San Miguel Church dominates the western half. The church's origi-

This plaza building, photographed in 1974, illustrates San Miguel del Vado's Southwest Vernacular architecture.

nal appearance has been masked by hard exterior plastering, modernization of the bell towers, the addition of remodeled, pointed Gothic arch windows, and the interior additions of a wood slat ceiling, wood and linoleum flooring, and modern doors.

Nevertheless, the building's origin as a mission church in 1811 is apparent in the building layout, the massive walls, and the twin adobe bell towers. The bottom ten feet of the church walls are made of red sandstone, while the upper portions are built of adobe, indicating that the builders of the church saw a need to protect the church from floods. North of the church there is a row of houses that probably date to the original construction of the plaza. Among traces of the foundations of a long string of rooms southwest of the church are fragments of ceramics and metals which suggest that this row of buildings may have served as the stopping or bartering point for traders on the Santa Fe Trail.

San José huddles on the opposite bank and just a mile upriver of San Miguel. A Parker Through-Truss bridge used to carry Route 66 traffic across the Pecos River here. The old bridge, its approaches long ago washed out, still stands at the river on the edge of San José, but a newer bridge upstream now directs traffic north of the village. A five-minute side trip from the rerouted highway affords an opportunity to see the bridge and this remarkable old town.

The residents of both San José and San Miguel were placed in possession of their lands within the San Miguel del Vado Land Grant in 1803, but the San José plaza has suffered less damage and its outlines are more clearly discernible. Most of the houses in San José show only modest signs of modern influence and the plaza conveys a feeling of how San Miguel—and many other plaza communities in New Mexico—might have appeared before it fell into decline. The church in the middle of the plaza, built in 1826, is an eloquent example of the church architecture from this period, which followed the decline of the Franciscan missionary effort in New Mexico.

**FORTRESS
AT THE GATEWAY:
PECOS AND
GLORIETA PASS**

Past San José, Route 66, finally on a westward course and parallel to railroad tracks again, took aim at Glorieta Pass. Here the route shadows ancient trading trails that funneled trade from the Plains toward the pass and on into the Rio Grande Valley—a trail that saw heavy use in Spanish Colonial days and in the Mexican and American territorial days as the Santa Fe Trail. From Romeroville on to Santa Fe, Route 66 stayed to this old trail. West of San José del Vado, it passed through the railroad town of Rowe and then by the ruins of **Pecos Pueblo**. Located on a rise between 7,000-foot Rowe Mesa and the 12,000-foot peaks of the Sangre de Cristo Mountains, the pueblo had a clear vantage on Glorieta Pass, the most important crossing between the Great Plains and the Rio Grande Valley. Pecos Pueblo was home to the only Pueblo people in the Pecos drainage at the time of Spanish contact. Since about A.D. 1450 it had controlled the vital trade routes through the pass, where the Rio Grande's agricultural bounty was swapped for buffalo meat and hides.

Pecos Pueblo's hegemony brought it great wealth and at the same time demanded a strong military presence. With the arrival of the Spanish, Pecos threw the force of its considerable resistance behind the Pueblo Revolt of

Pecos National Monument preserves a complex of sites inhabited from 800 to 1838 by Pueblo people.
Photograph by Fred Mang, Jr., 1967.

1680, which drove the Spanish colony from New Mexico. When the Spanish returned, however, Pecos's leaders split bitterly over the question of whether or not to form an alliance with them. Those in favor of cooperating with the conquerors won out and Pecos found itself in the unenviable position of buffer between increasingly hostile Indians of the plains and the Spanish towns of the Rio Grande Valley. The pueblo supplied Spanish military campaigns with hundreds of armed warriors to subdue other Indian groups, including the fearsome Comanches. By casting their lot with the European overlords, they earned the enmity of former trading partners on the plains as well as pueblos in the Rio Grande Valley—a rift that contributed to the decline of the Pecos Pueblo and its eventual abandonment in 1838.

The Pecos people had dealt with hostile neighbors for centuries, and their pueblo was highly defensive in plan. Its multistory room blocks were surrounded by a protective wall and enclosed a central plaza. Additional security came from a complete lack of ground-level doors; entry to all rooms was through openings in the ceiling. Ladders, easily retractable in times of siege, led to the rooftops, and others led down into individual rooms.

Franciscan missionaries oversaw Pueblo labor in the construction of a church at Pecos, completed between 1621 and 1625 and dedicated to Nuestra Señora de los Angeles. This massive edifice was one of the most impressive mission churches ever built in New Mexico. It measured 145 feet from doorway to altar, stood forty feet tall, and contained over 300,000 adobe bricks. Pueblo laborers hauled its giant vigas from miles away and formed the adobe bricks on site. Historian John L. Kessell describes it as "a sixteenth-century medieval fortress-church rendered in adobe in the baroque age at the ends of the earth." Kessell surmised the church's appearance from written descriptions and drawings, since the Pecos people destroyed the church, brick by brick, during the Pueblo Revolt. Until its foundations were discovered in 1967, the old structure was unknown and historians believed that an eighteenth-century church built on top of its foundations was the original church. The newer church—which was actually the fourth built at Pecos—resembled the many other churches built by the tribe under Franciscan control in the pre-revolt period: massive (though much smaller than the seventeenth-century church), cruciform in plan and adorned modestly with interior artwork, mostly created locally. It served the pueblo and surrounding Hispanic villages until a new church went up in San Miguel del Vado in 1804 and the priest transferred to the more populous Hispanic town.

The last survivors of Pecos Pueblo watched the first wagon trains labor down the Santa Fe Trail past their front door in 1821. Later travelers on the trail would often camp at the half-empty pueblo, whose residents sometimes joined them around the campfire. The Pueblo population had by then been reduced to a few and its former glory was forgotten. In 1838, the last twenty residents of this once-proud pueblo packed up and left, going to live with their Towa-speaking relatives on the other side of the Rio Grande Valley at Jemez Pueblo. The remaining walls of the mission church still stand sentinel at the pueblo, now witness to thousands of vehicles rushing to and from the pass on the four-lane interstate.

Architects of the Santa Fe style looked to the pueblos and their missions for inspiration, just as they had to Spanish villages of the region. Pecos was by then abandoned, but pueblos closer to Santa Fe were still inhabited, and Taos—also an important trade town at a mountain pass—retained a multistory structure similar to the fortress that had stood at Pecos. From these ancient building types, architects adopted irregular massing, multistory plans, and battered walls. Some also seized upon the rooftop ladders as a design element, and decorative ladders showed up on buildings adhering to the new styles. Such oddities as the placement of roof ladders on residences, gas stations, and fire stations seemed perfectly natural as the Santa Fe building styles spread in popularity throughout the Southwest.

Pecos National Monument maintains the extensive multi-layered ruins of Pecos Pueblo, including the partially reconstructed mission church. Nearby is Glorieta Battlefield, where the defeat of Confederates by soldiers from Fort Union and a group of Colorado volunteers ended the Confederate push to claim the western states. Pecos Park headquarters are situated astride old Route 66 just a few miles east of the Hispanic town of Pecos. This village came late in the Hispanic settlement scheme of the upper Pecos, as Spanish and Mexican colonists had previously avoided the area out of respect for the "one square league" rule of Pueblo land ownership—the stipulation in Spanish law that the Pueblos be granted ownership over lands extending for one-half league in the cardinal directions from the center of their villages. With the waning strength of Pecos Pueblo, encroachments by landless Hispanics became commonplace, and in 1824 a grant of Pecos land was given to a settler from Santa Fe. The Pecos people bitterly protested through all legal channels, but by the time the case was decided in their favor, it was a moot point: the Pecos were too few and decided to abandon their home. In their absence, the Hispanic town of Pecos sprang up on the illegal grant and took not only the land but the pueblo's name as well.

Pecos grew quickly on the overflow of Hispanics from the Rio Grande Valley and saw another growth spurt when mining boomed in the mountains nearby later in the century. Route 66 passed right through town starting in 1926, and local businesses set up shop to serve the stream of visitors. The Pecos Motor Company still stands on the south end of town, but few other remnants of the era remain.

Route 66 and Interstate 25 coincide through Glorieta Pass, running parallel to the railroad tracks, but at Cañoncito on the west side of the mountains, Route 66 diverges from the rails and interstate to aim toward Santa Fe. Ironically, the main line of the Atchison, Topeka and Santa Fe Railway didn't pass through Santa Fe—a fact that had enormous economic consequences for Santa Fe. Whereas Santa Fe had enjoyed primacy as New Mexico's largest town, the state capitol, and the terminus of the Santa Fe Trail, it lost its status when the rails went south through Albuquerque in 1880. The change sent Santa Fe into an economic depression that lasted until the second decade of the twentieth century. City leaders ended the decline by capitalizing on the golden opportunity to reinvent the town as "the City Different," its current slogan. Key to this makeover was the creation of a uniform architectural image for the town that would engender tourist interest while at the same time satisfying the yearnings of a new class of immigrants who came to Santa Fe seeking escape from the industrial landscapes and cities of the eastern U.S.

The new Museum of New Mexico, founded in 1917, was at the center of the movement to foist uniform building styles on the town's populace. To achieve their goals, the historic preservationists "methodically transformed [the city] into a harmonious Pueblo-Spanish fantasy through speculative restorations, the removal of overt signs of Americanization, and historic design review for new buildings," in the words of architectural historian Chris Wilson. They imitated and modified certain elements of colonial and Pueblo buildings to suit their own purposes and tastes. They used as prototypes New Mexico's informal Franciscan missions to distinguish Santa Fe's historical character from the Mission Revival style being cultivated in California at the time.

The styles promoted in Santa Fe were not without precedent, as architects had been experimenting with traditional forms in the Southwest since the end of the nineteenth century. Pseudo "pueblos" were common along the tourist tracks blazed by railroad tourism promoters and buildings at the University of New Mexico in

Albuquerque also revealed an early Pueblo style of architecture. But in Santa Fe, the tourism-motivated forms were refined, fused with local architectural traditions, and formalized beginning in 1912 in a city plan for Santa Fe. The new forms had a tremendous influence on regional building styles throughout the Southwest, from massive civic structures to motels.

THE PLAZA DIFFERENT: DOWNTOWN SANTA FE

Route 66 entered Santa Fe along the former path of the Santa Fe Trail, following the street with the same name. Nowadays the sprawl of town covers the foothills of the Sangre de Cristo Mountains, but in the 1920s and '30s these hills were bare of housing, and today's pricey home lots occupied the outskirts of the sleepy town of 11,000 inhabitants, most of them Hispanic. Cruising down the Santa Fe Trail as it neared the plaza, drivers in the 1930s passed by humble architecture and through neighborhoods in the midst of radical transformation. Earlier visitors to Santa Fe derided the adobe architecture of the dusty town, but by the time Route 66 was designated in 1926, the romanticization of adobe was in full swing. Simple abodes that once looked like those in the Pecos Valley were being renovated and conspicuously styled, while new structures were being built to resemble isolated, mini-pueblos. Some adobe fantasy homes included actual pieces of structures from outlying Hispanic and Pueblo villages. One such house, designed by the indefatigable John Gaw Meem, included beams scavenged from the church in Las Trampas, the Pueblo ruins of Gran Quivira, and homes in San Miguel del Vado, Acoma Pueblo, and Bernalillo.

Following Old Santa Fe Trail to the very heart of Santa Fe, Route 66 passed within view of some of downtown's most significant architectural

San Miguel Church in Santa Fe was the colonial capital's first parish church. It was rebuilt after the Pueblo Revolt of 1680 and has a rich and complex history.

The former DeVargas
Hotel, now the
Hotel St. Francis,
in the heart of Santa Fe.

monuments. Its path took it directly in front of the **San Miguel Church**. Built around 1645 and remodeled in 1710, San Miguel's bell tower was remodeled in the 1950s with its lines clearly emulating the tower at the La Fonda Hotel. After crossing the Santa Fe River, the route led drivers by the front doors of a church of totally different conception: the chapel at Loretto Academy, which departs radically from almost all other buildings in town in materials and style. The 1878 Gothic Revival style chapel, modeled on Saint Chapelle in Paris, was made of locally cut stone and resembled its adobe neighbors only in its muted brown coloration. Its construction was inspired by Jean Baptiste Lamy, who was appointed by the church to the New Mexico Territory in 1850.

From the corner of Water Street and Old Santa Fe Trail, where Route 66 turned west, travelers could see the imposing mass of the **La Fonda Hotel** one block away on the southeast corner of the plaza. Designed in 1919 by the architectural firm Rapp, Rapp and Hendrickson, inspiration for the multi-leveled hotel came in part from Taos Pueblo. A major addition to the hotel designed by John Gaw Meem in 1927 added the six-story tower. Few would have noticed then that the tower looked very much like the twin bell towers at the Acoma Pueblo mission sixty miles west of Albuquerque. The similarity was no coincidence: Meem was in the midst of redesigning Acoma's towers during a reconstruction of the mission. He conceived them based in large measure on his own concept of what they should look like, since no photographs or drawings of the originals existed. After using the tower design at La Fonda and Acoma Mission, he adapted it for other, smaller churches at Acoma. It would be imitated again during a restoration of the San Miguel Church in Santa Fe.

San Francisco Street looking east toward the Cathedral. La Fonda Hotel can be seen on the south corner, photographed in 1926.

A stroll up to the plaza allowed a view up San Francisco Street to Archbishop Lamy's second architectural legacy, the **St. Francis Cathedral**. Like the Loretto Chapel, the cathedral's design differs drastically from the rest of the buildings downtown. Lamy recruited Italian stonemasons and French architects to build the Byzantine–Romanesque Revival church. Made of the same kind of local stone as the chapel, the new cathedral literally engulfed Santa Fe's old adobe church, the Parroquia, leaving it as a side altar in the overarching cathedral. The symbolism in Lamy's move was clear: the newer, more European order of things would simply overwhelm and absorb the "primitive," indigenous forms. The imposition couldn't erase the local populace's faith, however. The small colonial-era church is still accessible and serves as an important touchstone for Hispanic residents of Santa Fe, who continue their devotion to the chapel's primary icon, Nuestra Señora del Rosario, also known as La Conquistadora—Our Lady of the Conquest.

Crossing to the north side of the plaza, the visitor in the 1930s could inspect the Palace of the Governors, the seat of Spanish Colonial and Mexican governments for 236 years preceding the American takeover of the state. This building had been transformed early in the renascence of Santa Fe by a young archaeologist/photographer in the employ of the Museum of New Mexico, Jesse Nusbaum. He initiated this, the first serious restoration of a historical Santa Fe structure, in 1919. As part of the cadre that was striving to re-create Santa Fe's image, he introduced significant changes to the Governor's palace in an effort to emphasize qualities he associated with Spanish influences while at the same time eliminating effects of Americanization. The resulting structure's portal is supported by posts much larger than those seen in old photos of the building and is topped with a heavy parapet to further give it a massive, "palace-like" stature. Upon its completion, the Palace exerted a strong influence on the emerging Santa Fe style.

Just down Palace Avenue, the **Museum of Fine Arts**, completed in 1915, represented another early expression of the Santa Fe style with a strong integration of Spanish and Pueblo styles. Vigas and canales protrude from its multistory Pueblo forms, and the two mission facades at opposite corners are patterned principally after the mission church at Acoma, with some additional influence from the mission churches at San Felipe, Laguna, and Cochiti Pueblos. Inside the museum, the St. Francis auditorium replicated the interior of a mission church, complete with carved vigas and corbels and elegant herringbone latillas.

While those busy redefining Santa Fe were eliminating evidence of American influences at every turn, some design elements that came with Americanization persisted and were in fact eventually deemed acceptable contributions to the Santa Fe style. Buildings on the west and east sides of the plaza show these details well. The newcomers on the Santa Fe Trail had brought milled lumber to the territory, and carpenters busied themselves remaking portals using squared beams in place of round pine logs. In deference to the Greek Revival movement that had been popular in the Midwest and eastern U.S. at one time, they adorned these posts with molding at top and bottom meant to resemble the capitals and bases of Greek columns. The milled lumber was also employed to trim out windows with frames meant to

This 1918 photograph of the Museum of Fine Arts in Santa Fe, on the plaza, shows a wood vendor's wagon.
Photograph by Wesley Bradfield.

resemble Greek columns, entablatures, and pediments. All the new woodwork was whitewashed so that it stood out handsomely from the rich brown adobe walls. Fired brick also came west with the Americans and found a place in local buildings. Because of the expense of hauling the bricks over the Santa Fe Trail, they were used at first only for fireplaces and to cap adobe walls to protect them from the weather. Masons sometimes laid the brick cornices to resemble Greek dentil courses.

Such territorial elements were at first explicitly excluded from definitions of Santa Fe style, but beginning in the 1930s some architects began to employ these countrified Greek Revival touches deliberately. In doing so, John Gaw Meem and his associate Gordon Street developed the Territorial Revival style and brought it to full expression in the Federal Emergency Recovery Administration building (now the Villagra building) in 1934 and the Supreme Court building in 1936. These two impressive structures were finished in the last years that Route 66 came through Santa Fe, standing side by side on the south side of the Santa Fe River within plain view. At the time, the state capitol, neoclassical in design, stood out in stark contrast to the new buildings and the rest of Santa Fe, but local architects Willard Kruger and Kenneth Clark brought the building into harmony by removing the capitol dome and temple-front entry and remodeling the structure in Territorial Revival style in 1950. Territorial Revival became the unofficial style of the official New Mexico and, along with the other expressions of Santa Fe style, became popular regionally.

In 1966, a new capitol would be built south of its predecessor. It generated extreme controversy when its abstract modernist form was first proposed. The Kruger firm, designer of the capitol, distanced itself from the implicit modernism in the building, claiming that the circular floor plan imitated the round kivas, or ceremonial structures, found in some of the pueblos. Traditionalists and regionalists remained unconvinced, and Kruger was forced to consult John Gaw Meem to redesign the building's facades. Meem added Territorial style elements to bring the round, two-story building into line with the accepted styles for Santa Fe.

Beyond the site of the 1950 capitol, Route 66 turned onto Galisteo Street, crossed the Santa Fe River, and passed in front of the DeVargas Hotel (now the Hotel St. Francis). This handsome two-story building was built in 1880 as an adjacent private residence and boarding house. It was rehabilitated in the 1920s, following on the heels of the renovation of La Fonda Hotel, with its two parts joined to form a luxury hotel in Mission Revival style.

FANTASY FRANCHISES: SANTA FE'S ADOBE STRIP

After a short jog on Galisteo, the route veered south onto Cerrillos Road, the primary north-south thoroughfare that led out of town toward Albuquerque. On the outskirts of town it passed in front of the School for the Deaf—a multistory building designed by Rapp, Rapp and Hendrickson in 1917 that strongly emphasized Pueblo elements—continuing past the Santa Fe Indian School and the Indian Hospital, also built in Pueblo style. Beyond these institutions, Route 66 followed Santa Fe's modest commercial strip—the beginnings of the seemingly endless succession of pseudo-adobe buildings that today persists to the edge of town. Here the phenomenon of Santa Fe style spilled from structures and neighborhoods out onto a commercial strip of buildings with no connection to Santa Fe's past. From donut shops to shopping malls to car washes, the earth-toned walls and protruding vigas compete with neon along the crowded boulevard. Several tourist courts remain along Cerrillos Road, including the El Rey Court (now the El Rey Inn). Built in 1936, the El Rey took the form of a classic auto court and included a filling station and carports (enclosed in the 1950s or '60s) in between motel rooms. Other tourist courts on Cerrillos Road past the School date from the 1940s, after Route 66 had been rerouted away from Santa Fe, including the King's Rest Court, the Western Scene, and Cottonwood Court

Once beyond Santa Fe, Route 66 coincided with US Highway 85 to roughly follow the course of the Camino Real, or Royal Road, that in colonial days connected Santa Fe with Chihuahua and, ultimately, Mexico City. From the outskirts of Santa Fe for the next thirty miles, Interstate 25 has largely subsumed old Route 66, and the old road is accessible only for short sections. About fifteen miles from town, Route 66 came to the lip of a high volcanic escarpment known as **La Bajada**, or "the descent," where east-west trending basalt cliffs drop 500 feet from the Caja del Rio plateau to the lower Rio Grande Valley. Wayfarers in New Mexico have long been aware of this dramatic natural boundary, which divides the Rio Grande Valley neatly into northern and southern sections. Spanish authorities recognized the escarpment as an important divide and in 1660 formally designated two subprovinces within New Mexico—the Rio Arriba (Upper River) and the Rio Abajo (Lower River).

Route 66 followed the Camino Real (Royal Road) down the precipice of La Bajada south of Santa Fe cutting down the slope in numerous switchbacks that dropped 500 feet in just two miles. In 1932, the route was redirected three miles to the east and the old switchbacks fell into disuse.
Photograph by Sam Hudelson, ca. 1928.

Route 66 followed a slightly different course than the Camino Real down the precipice of **La Bajada**, cutting down the slope in twenty-six switchbacks that dropped the full 500 feet in just two miles. The previous road, built by the Army in the 1860s, dropped down La Bajada at a dizzying 28 percent grade. In 1908 laborers from Cochiti Pueblo toiled alongside inmates from the state penitentiary to carve the new path into the slope. Upon completion in 1922 it was regarded as an engineering feat. Even at its much reduced, 8 percent grade, this small stretch of Route 66 was surely the most dramatic—and to many, frightening—in all of New Mexico. A sign at the top of La Bajada warned: "This road is not fool proof, but safe for a sane driver."

Santo Domingo Trading Post, built in 1880, is the oldest trading post on Route 66. A new trading post adjacent to the original was built by the Seligman family in the Mission Revival style in 1922. Signs covering the structure exclaimed "Visit, Watch, Trade with Real Indians" and "JFK was here!" The post operated until 1995 but was destroyed by fire in February 2001.

Photographed ca. 1954.

Route 66 was redirected three miles to the east in 1932 (to approximately the present location of Interstate 25) and the old switchbacks fell into disuse, although it's still possible to traverse them on foot. The vantage at the top of the switchbacks affords spectacular views of the upper and lower Rio Grande Valley, and near the edge of the mesa one can still see painted lettering on the basalt rocks announcing the Santa Fe auto camp. At the bottom, a bridge made of creosote-treated lumber, completed in 1927 as part of the initial Route 66 construction, crosses the Santa Fe River. The frame-and-stucco cabins still standing at the base of La Bajada offered rustic accommodations to Route 66 travelers. This simple sort of overnight lodging was the first type to develop along the highway. The cabins at La Bajada today represent one of only two remaining examples of the freestanding cabin era on the old highway.

From the bottom of La Bajada, Route 66 shadowed the route of the Camino Real southward past Cochiti Pueblo, which has always been isolated from the main travel routes because of its location on the opposite, west side of the Rio Grande. Route 66 rejoined the railway corridor—from which it had diverged at Cañoncito east of Santa Fe—just a few miles north of Santo

Domingo Pueblo at the **Santo Domingo Trading Post**. The first incarnation of the post was built at the site in 1880 by the German-Jewish Seligman family, which built a new trading post building adjacent to the original in 1922 and claimed the complex as the oldest trading post on Route 66. The Seligmans managed the trading post along with mercantile stores in several New Mexico communities, including Bernalillo and Santa Fe. The Santo Domingo post served an eclectic clientele, including residents of Santo Domingo Pueblo, passengers stopping at the nearby Domingo Depot of the Santa Fe Railway, and, starting in 1926, travelers on Route 66 and US 85. Although the number of patrons dropped when the highway was relocated three miles east in 1932, the trading post continued to operate until 1995 and the building stood until February 2001, when it was destroyed by fire.

South of the trading post, Route 66 veered to the southeast, steering clear of the pueblo. Continuing southeastward from Santo Domingo, Route 66 traversed

The Big Cut, still visible from southbound Interstate 25, was vaunted as a feat of modern engineering when its cut-and-fill construction was completed in 1909 as part of New Mexico's Route 1. Route 66 traffic passed through the Big Cut from 1926 to 1931.
Photograph by Anna L. Hase, ca. 1928.

The Iceberg Café was located at several sites in Albuquerque before being moved in the 1950s to Bernalillo's main street, the former Route 66 before its realignment in 1937. Photograph by Russell Lee, ca. 1940.

Our Lady of Sorrows Church, originally constructed in 1857 in the central New Mexico agricultural town of Bernalillo, is an excellent example of nineteenth-century ecclesiastical architecture. Combining features of the preceding Spanish and Mexican periods with elements brought to the area by French-born Catholic bishop Jean Baptiste Lamy, this impressive adobe structure displays elements of Spanish Colonial and Gothic Revival styles. Cobb Studio Collection, ca. 1880.

sandy foothills and deep arroyos on a course that aimed toward the uplifted fault block of the Sandia Mountains. After entering San Felipe Pueblo land and crossing a giant wash known as Tonque Arroyo—now the site of San Felipe's thriving roadside casino—the highway climbed to a conspicuous, deep notch in an alluvial ridge. The Big Cut, still visible from southbound Interstate 25, was vaunted as a feat of modern engineering when its cut-and-fill construction was completed in 1909 as part of New Mexico's Route 1. Route 66 traffic passed through the Big Cut from 1926 until the road was rerouted a half-mile to the west in 1931. The cut, although only eighteen feet wide and about seventy-five feet long, is a striking reminder of how early road engineers solved difficult road-building problems.

Once through the Big Cut, Route 66 angled back toward the Rio Grande and rejoined the railroad tracks at Algodones, just south of Ranchitos, a community within Santa Ana Pueblo (also a Keresan-speaking pueblo). Here, it's possible to drive the old route again as it passes through farmlands watered by irrigation ditches that draw off the Rio Grande. A few miles past Santa Ana, the road leaves the boundaries of Indian land for the first time since descending La Bajada and comes into **Bernalillo**, a town mentioned in Spanish Colonial documents in 1696. Founded by Hispanic farmers and sheep ranchers, Bernalillo now sits at the crossroads of two major highways, NM 44 (technically US 550, which terminates in Bernalillo along NM 44) and Interstate 25.

HARD-EDGED ADOBE: ABENICIO SALAZAR HISTORIC DISTRICT

It's hard to make out the old core of Bernalillo amid the clutter of roadside businesses, new housing, and mobile homes spreading out from the crossroads, but just a few blocks after crossing US 550, across the street from the **Our Lady of Sorrows Church**, a small neighborhood provides a fairly accurate representation of the old town. Its many historic buildings, including several school buildings associated with the church, adjacent agricultural land, and residential structures, have been formally recognized as the **Abenicio Salazar Historic District**.

The Abenicio Salazar Historic District is representative of old-town Bernalillo.

Abenicio Salazar, a local builder who lived from 1857 to 1941, crafted the largest adobe buildings in the area, including the Our Lady of Sorrows High School. Salazar also built the local flour mill, a winery, a firewall for the lumber mill, most of the buildings in the entire coal-mining town of Hagan east of Bernalillo, and numerous local houses. Straight walls and square corners characterize Salazar's buildings. He used adobe plastered with cement to achieve a scale rarely found in adobe construction. The high school building is the only one of Salazar's large structures that survives in good condition.

The Sisters of Loretto, who had founded a girls' grade school in Bernalillo in 1874, also started the high school and operated it from its opening in 1923 until 1970. The high school building is the largest and most prominent structure in the historic district, apart from the church. The square two-story high school building has a flat roof and stands directly across old Route 66 from the twin spires of the church. A Pueblo Revival-styled stepped parapet, capped with concrete, tops the building on all four sides, and a rounded arch of unglazed brick—another hallmark of Salazar's work—frames the main entrance. Inside the building, broad hallways run the length of the building on both floors. Two large staircases with elaborate wooden banisters and paneled casings lead to the second story, where large rooms with fifteen-foot ceilings, large double-hung windows, and pressed-metal ceilings all remain remarkably intact.

As if in counterpoint to the strongly vertical high school, the Our Lady of Sorrows Convent to the north strikes a horizontal profile, although it, too, is square in plan. José Leandro Perea built the convent from adobe bricks for the Sisters of Loretto in 1874. The ten-room, patio-centered building served as a private school run by the sisters. The four sides of the building enclose a courtyard with a portal extending around three sides. The roof is now flat, although for many years it had a metal-covered gable roof. In balanced symmetry, a door is located in the center of each of the four sides of the building, each door topped by a shaped lintel.

Many other buildings of historical and architectural interest still stand in this small neighborhood. Some of the most conspicuous and best maintained owe their preservation to their association with the school, long a stable feature of the neighborhood. The buildings in the school complex, including the former convent and the former high school (now the Convent Gallery), are collectively referred to as El Zocalo complex.

A mile past the Abenicio Salazar historic district, Route 66 passes through modern, downtown Bernalillo—the seat of Sandoval County—and in another few blocks enters the town's old downtown neighborhood. In less than a mile, the roadside jumble of housing and businesses stops suddenly, as the highway enters Sandia Pueblo land. The road continues south, hugging the edge of irrigated farmland of the reservation. The impressive west face of the Sandia range hangs over the valley, its summit regarded as a sacred spot for the people of nearby pueblo.

**IN THE
COTTONWOOD
HEART OF THE
RIO ABAJO:
ALAMEDA TO
ALBUQUERQUE**

After a commercial-free hiatus of seven miles on Pueblo land, Route 66 becomes Fourth Street and enters Alameda, where old adobe houses and small farms are slowly ceding ground to new residential and business developments, their growth fanned by the explosive growth of Albuquerque. In the early 1700s, Alameda took root as a community separate from Albuquerque, claiming ground that had been the site of a Tiwa Pueblo abandoned a century before. Alameda means "cottonwood grove," a name that would have been appropriate to any locale along this stretch of the Middle Rio Grande, home to the Southwest's largest and least disturbed riparian forest. Although overtones of the town's rural past still resonate—and provide fodder for real estate brochures aimed at urbanites seeking escape—Alameda is essentially one of several suburbs in Albuquerque's North Valley. For the next nine miles, neighborhoods along Route 66 are made up of a combination of older rural homes, many made of adobe and reflecting Southwest Vernacular style, and more modern homes and businesses, most of which self-consciously emulate popular Pueblo Revival and Territorial regional styles.

As Fourth Street nears the high-rise cluster of buildings that marks downtown, it passes under the roaring thoroughfare of Interstate 40, now New Mexico's major east-west travel corridor—a distinction that once belonged to Fourth Street/Route 66, where nineteen tourist courts were located in 1937. Only two are still in business: the El Camino Motor Hotel and the King's Rest, now the Interstate Inn. With the construction of the Central Street bridge, Route 66 was rerouted and Fourth Street lost east- and westbound traffic. Its primacy for north-south travel was diminished when downtown redevelopment closed off the street at Marquette Street just shy of Central Avenue. To get to the junction of Central and Fourth—the only place where Route 66, in its two alignments, essentially crossed itself—now requires a jog around downtown.

**OLDER THAN
OLD TOWN:
THE BARELAS/
SOUTH FOURTH
HISTORIC DISTRICT**

When Route 66 visitors came to downtown Albuquerque in the 1920s and '30s, they found a diversity of building types, including the most modern styles and multistory structures befitting New Mexico's only blossoming urban center. Many of Central Avenue's old brick buildings suffered a long decline after World War II, but in recent years many have been restored. (See the next chapter, "Touring Moriarty and Albuquerque".)

In 1926 the highway continued south beyond Central Avenue and entered one of Albuquerque's oldest neighborhoods. Now known as the Barelas/South Fourth Street Historic District, this combination residential and commercial neighborhood contains buildings of architectural and historical significance representing three waves of Albuquerque development.

A rancher named Pedro Varela (alternatively spelled "Barela") maintained an *estancia* at a ford of the Rio Grande one mile south of the plaza in this area in 1662, long before Albuquerque was founded. The town, the last of three in New Mexico to be designated as a *villa,* was sited in 1706 because of its proximity to the river crossing. A farming village sprouted along the Camino Real between the plaza and the river, and by 1860, three hundred farmers living along the road drew water from the Barelas Acequia to irrigate their crops. A cluster of adobe houses with metal roofs and a neighborhood grocery store at the intersection of Fourth Street and Barelas Road represent the modern remnants of this old community.

Under a subsidiary company, the Atchison, Topeka, and Santa Fe Railway platted the town of New Albuquerque in 1885. Construction of a roundhouse and major locomotive repair shops made Albuquerque a regional railroad maintenance center. The economic boom fueled the city for decades, but the rails were a mixed blessing for the residents of the Barelas neighborhood. They brought employment opportunities but at the same time the tracks bisected the neighborhood's farm fields, separating the acequia from the bulk of the farmland and leaving farmers unable to water their land. Farmers from Barelas became mechanics and laborers for the railroad, joined by job seekers from Hispanic villages of Northern New Mexico as well as immigrants from Mexico, Germany, and the eastern U.S.

As demand for housing rose quickly, developers platted speculative subdivisions in the Barelas neighborhood, which became home to nearly 1,500 inhabitants by 1920. These subdivisions took an unusual form, however, as they had to be squeezed onto long, narrow family fields—a pattern consequent to the tradition of dividing land equally among heirs and leaving each with access to the irrigation ditch. The long lots of farmland led to blocks of unequal width and properties that extended unequal distances back from the roadways.

At the north end of Barelas, a new type of architecture began to replace the older homes in the nineteen-teens. In place of adobes in the Southwest Vernacular style, houses of brick or wood-frame construction appeared with gable or hipped roofs or multiple intersecting roof planes. In contrast to Santa Fe, builders in Albuquerque didn't have to contend with a city plan and political leaders who were advocating a standardization of building styles, and as a result all kinds of new building plans infiltrated the Barelas neighborhood, from simple shotgun houses and four-square houses to modest Queen Anne-style houses and, later, bungalows. Many of these buildings are still standing and retain their design characteristics. Fourth Street was not yet a through street and most commercial development was taking place on Second Street, closer to the locomotive shops.

A second burst of growth began in the Barelas neighborhood when Fourth Street was extended to Bridge Street in 1924 and became part of New Mexico Route 1, the road that was also known by the redundant name the "Camino Real Highway." Tourist courts began to appear along the road, although most of them were located farther south along South Fourth Street, now Isleta Road, where land was cheaper. Within the district, commercial ventures multiplied and South Fourth Street became the commercial center of Barelas, catering primarily to local residents and farmers coming to town with their produce.

The commercialization of the district continued through the Great Depression and wasn't slowed even when the Central Avenue bridge diverted traffic from Fourth Street in 1931 or when Route 66 was realigned to Central in 1937. In keeping with the modernization of the city, many new business ventures built structures in white Streamline Moderne style, which set a new, progressive image for the Central Avenue strip. After a hiatus during World War II, growth resumed full force and continued apace until around 1947. Businessmen continued to invest in new and larger retail outlets. The Streamline Moderne image of the district still held sway but gradually the more angular International style began to make inroads in commercial buildings.

By the mid-1930s, the Barelas-Fourth Street shopping district superseded Old Town as the leading Hispanic shopping district in Albuquerque. It reached its commercial peak in the 1950s. Yet even as it peaked, the seeds of the district's demise had been sown. Longtime Barelas families began to succumb, along with downtown businesses, to the irresistible pull of the suburbs. The local economy suffered a serious blow in the early 1950s when the Santa Fe Railway converted its locomotives to diesel power, which required less maintenance, and consolidated repairs in Texas and California. An urban renewal project relocated one-third of the families living south of Bridge Street to the South Valley or into the Northeast Heights. Finally, the closure of Fourth Street at the Albuquerque civic plaza in 1974 cut off north-south through traffic on Fourth Street.

City and neighborhood leaders are working to revitalize the Barelas/South Fourth Street Historic District. The National Hispanic Cultural Center, opened in 2000 at the south end of the district, is a centerpiece of this renewal, which also includes streetscape improvements and the construction of new

Route 66 crosses the Rio Grande at the Barelas bridge, photographed in 1931.

parks. The city offers assistance to property owners for façade and building restoration to help maintain the district's historic character, and the Main Street Program offers design assistance. The city purchased the pivotal Red Ball Café building and resold it at a reduced price with guarantees of renovation. Collectively, these efforts may help restore some luster to the neighborhood and help it gain the recognition it deserves as an important historical neighborhood and the most intact first-generation automobile strip in Albuquerque.

BACK IN THE BOSQUE: THE SOUTH VALLEY TO ISLETA

Fourth Street ends at Bridge Street (now Avenida César Chávez), where Route 66 turns right and reaches the Rio Grande in less than a mile. Across the bridge, the route turns left to coincide with Isleta Boulevard, where traces of old tourist courts remain standing. As the road runs through the suburban neighborhoods of Albuquerque's South Valley—some of them of the same vintage as the Barelas neighborhood and all of them predominantly Hispanic—the commercial development very slowly declines and the surroundings become more rural. Just seven miles from the bridge the road once again travels through open farmland with sparse housing. An abandoned trading post on the left side of the road signals the approaching Indian land. After passing under Interstate 25, the route comes upon signs marking the boundary of Isleta Pueblo lands. Just as the Sandia Pueblo lands create an open space buffer north of Albuquerque, Isleta creates a largely commercial-free zone on the city's south margin, excepting a casino to the east and golf course to the west. These two large tracts of land, strictly off-limits to non-Indian ownership and development, have had the additional effect of squeezing Albuquerque the only direction it can grow—to the west, across the Rio Grande and up the West Mesa.

On its way to Los Lunas, Route 66 grazed the eastern edge of **Isleta Pueblo**, which is the southernmost and most populous Tiwa-speaking pueblo in New Mexico. The homes at Isleta huddle close around the village's main plaza, but outside this core homes are scattered more widely than in other pueblos. Fray Atanasio Dominguez noted the dispersed nature of settlement at Isleta when he traveled through New Mexico in 1776—a tendency that may reflect the Isletas' desire to be near their fields, which are larger and closer to the plaza here than at most other pueblos. The habit continues today, making Isleta the largest of all the pueblos in terms of areal extent.

The older houses surrounding the old plaza appear much today as they did in 1881, when Lt. John G. Burke visited the pueblo and observed one-storied adobes, with doors opening on the ground level. Frame windows and doors had already begun to replace the traditional roof entries, and selenite covered window openings. Larger windows of plate glass came later. Burke also commented on the numerous *hornos*—rounded ovens made of adobe introduced by the Spanish but quickly adopted by all the pueblos—that are still in evidence throughout the pueblo. The pueblo's large ceremonial *kiva* also still stands south of the main plaza, and its massive adobe church, originally dedicated to San Antonio de Padua, dominates the north side of the old plaza. Its construction in 1613 makes it second in age only to the San Esteban Mission at Acoma.

Isleta alone among the New Mexico pueblos did not join in the Pueblo Revolt of 1680. In fact, 1,500 Spanish settlers from the southern part of the province gathered there for safety after the rebels' initial attack. Many of the pueblo's residents joined the retreat to El Paso when the Spanish ceded the province to the insurgents. The Isletas made El Paso del Norte their new home, and their descendants live in the Texas border town today. When Don Diego de Vargas marched up the Rio Grande in 1692 to reclaim New Mexico for Spain, he reported that the partially burned walls of the church's nave were standing in the middle of the pueblo. These walls were probably used when Franciscan missionaries took up residence at the pueblo once again and organized a reconstruction of the church and the large *convento* adjoining it on the east in 1709-1710. When it was completed, the friars dedicated the new church to San Agustín, since the Isletas who fled south had taken with them their devotion to San Antonio.

There have been many modifications to San Agustín Mission since the

Route 66 borders the eastern edge of Isleta Pueblo on Albuquerque's southern perimeter. Although Pueblo Indian architecture has been modified by subsequent styles of construction, the massive adobe church of San Agustín, built in 1613, still dominates the landscape.
Photograph of church by Richard Federici, 1973.

Franciscans rebuilt it. The most obvious changes to the facade came with the addition of massive buttresses of adobe and stone on both sides of the front entrance in 1900. (Four buttresses were added to the west wall about the same time.) A walkway with a veranda roof and railing ran across the facade, resting on top of the buttresses, but it was removed in the mid-1930s and replaced in 1959 with a parapet. The belfries have undergone numerous alterations since Dominguez's visit in 1776. The padre had noted two adobe turrets on the front corners of the church, one containing a bell, but these had crumbled by 1881 and were replaced by a succession of new roof structures over the years. In 1959, Pueblo-style belfries were added to the corners and the low adobe arch where the bell now hangs was constructed in the middle of the facade.

Just as most homeowners in New Mexico were taking advantage of metal roofs, a pitched roof of corrugated iron went up over the church's flat roof in 1910. The new roof completely blocked light from the transverse clerestory window—a feature common to most Franciscan churches—that once illuminated the altar, but the 1959 restorations removed the pitched roof and restored the clerestory. Plank flooring, laid in place when milled lumber became available after Americanization, replaced the earth floor in the early 1900s. Many of the forty carved and corbelled vigas in the church date from the 1710 renovation, although the overlying latillas have been replaced.

Isleta prospered through the eighteenth and nineteenth centuries, producing abundant crops on water irrigated by the Rio Grande. In the 1870s the pueblo's population was augmented with the arrival of dissidents from Laguna Pueblo, a Keresan pueblo to the west. The Lagunas, led by the pueblo's *cacique*, or religious leader, had been locked in conflict with a progressive Protestant element at their pueblo and brought with them to Isleta some sacred objects, including kachinas. The kachina cult had been lost at Isleta, and the pueblo's leaders recognized that the Lagunas might help them rekindle their old tradition. Accordingly, they granted the Lagunas refuge and a tract of land at Isleta. A conservative faction later returned to Laguna, but some stayed at Isleta, where their descendants still live and speak their Keres language.

For a time this concrete bridge, photographed in 1922, was the only one to cross the Rio Grande, forcing auto enthusiasts to travel through Los Lunas until Route 66 was rerouted in 1937. A new bridge spanning the Rio Grande at Old Town in 1931 and another straddling the Rio Puerco in 1933 allowed for the construction of the road west of Albuquerque.

PAST THE PATRÓN'S CASA AND OUT OF THE RIFT: LOS LUNAS TO CORREO

Leaving Isleta, Route 66 continued south through the farmlands of the 200,000-acre reservation, leaving its bounds about eight miles from the pueblo plaza and slipping into **Los Lunas**, one of the fastest growing towns in New Mexico because of in-migration from the Albuquerque area. The town is named after the Luna family, which settled here in 1692 on a land grant—about the same time that the Otero family established Belen just to the south. These powerful families amassed land, livestock, and political power. With intermarriages in the 1800s, a dynasty was formed that controlled most of the southern Albuquerque basin. The

The Tranquilino Luna
Mansion, once home
to a powerful family,
is now a restaurant.
Architecturally, it is
remarkable for its
Victorian details and
adobe construction both.
Constructed in the early
1880s, it is considered
the best example of an
adobe Victorian residence
in New Mexico.
Photograph by Horace G.
Thomas II.

families initially built their fortune on sheep raising but also developed commercial interests and played key roles in the government of the New Mexico Territory, becoming the *patrones,* or political bosses, of the region.

Just after Route 66 turned west, it passed by a house belonging to the Luna-Otero clan that ostentatiously recalls the family's wealth. Its white-pillared portico suggests the grandeur of the southern plantation home and makes the building stand out conspicuously even today, when the house is surrounded by modern roads and brightly lit businesses. Known variously as the **Tranquilino Luna home,** the Luna Mansion, or the Luna-Otero Mansion, it is remarkable from an architectural standpoint because of its Victorian styling and adobe construction. It is the best example of an adobe Victorian residence in New Mexico and has retained most of its original design.

The fourteen-room house is built of large, flat slabs of sod called *terrones* set on a foundation of stone mortared with adobe. Cut from the Rio Grand floodplain, adobe *terrones* were used in New Mexico wherever there was abundant marshy bottomland, and few structures—and none of the stature of the Luna Mansion—remain. The flamboyant, two-story portico supported by four white pillars on the street-facing side of the house dates from early in the twentieth century, when it replaced a smaller and much simpler, single-story wooden front porch. A classical frieze containing paired Italianate brackets and center panels is repeated on all four sides of the rectangular house as well as on the square kitchen attached to the rear. The large bay windows on the north and east sides of the Luna house also stand out boldly and have been modified only slightly. Most destructive to the place's historical value is the nearby presence of commercial buildings and busy streets.

From Los Lunas, Route 66 angles northwest, following the route of New Mexico's Highway 6. The
highway parallels the railroad tracks across the Rio
Puerco and up the Rio San José to Correo, where it
crosses the San José River on an old Parker Through-Truss bridge, built in
1934 on a much smaller scale than the Rio Puerco bridge. Here, the long
diversion of the prealignment course of Route 66 comes to an end, and the
highway resumes a westward course toward California.

**The Los Lunas–Gallup
Road, ca. 1915.**

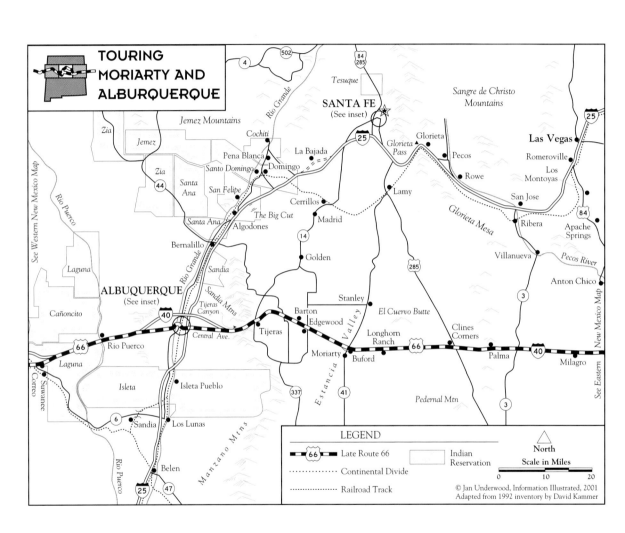

TOURING MORIARTY AND ALBURQUERQUE

Jemez Mountains

Sangre de Christo Mountains

See Western New Mexico Map

Zia

Jemez

Zia

Santa Ana

San Felipe

Rio Grande

Rio Puerco

Cochiti

Pena Blanca

Santo Domingo

Santa Ana

Algodones

The Big Cut

Bernalillo

Rio Grande

Sandia

La Bajada

Domingo

Cerrillos

Madrid

SANTA FE
(See inset)

Glorieta Pass

Tesuque

Glorieta

Pecos

Rowe

Lamy

Glorieta Mesa

Las Vegas

Romeroville

Los Montoyas

San Jose

Ribera

Apache Springs

Pecos River

Anton Chico

ALBUQUERQUE
(See inset)

Laguna

Cañoncito

Sandia Mtns

Tijeras Canyon

Golden

Stanley

Villanueva

Central Ave.

Tijeras

Barton

Edgewood

Moriarty

Buford

El Cuervo Butte

Longhorn Ranch

Clines Corners

Palma

Milagro

Rio Puerco

Laguna

Suwanee
Correo

Isleta

Isleta Pueblo

Sandia

Los Lunas

Manzano Mtns

Estancia Valley

Pedernal Mtn

See Eastern New Mexico Map

Rio Puerco

Belen

LEGEND

━66━ Late Route 66

.... Continental Divide

······ Railroad Track

Indian Reservation

North

Scale in Miles

0   10   20

© Jan Underwood, Information Illustrated, 2001
Adapted from 1992 inventory by David Kammer

TOUR THREE

TOURING MORIARTY
AND
ALBUQUERQUE

**THROUGH
THE GAP FROM
THE PINTO BEAN
CAPITAL TO
THE DUKE CITY**

Traversing New Mexico on Route 66 in the 1920s and '30s brought many striking changes in topography, but none more dramatic than the transition from the relative flatlands of the Great Plains to the mountains-and-valleys terrain of the Basin and Range. The distant bumps on the western horizon that had presaged an impending change for miles loomed as full-fledged mountain ranges by the time the road reached Moriarty. It became clear by then that the mountain mass to the west consisted of two ranges, the Sandias to the northwest and the Manzanos to the southwest. Gazing at the blue mountains from the Estancia Basin at Moriarty, the passage through this barrier that reaches over 10,000 feet in elevation isn't at all obvious. Finding a way through posed enormous challenges to road builders and permanently stymied railroad engineers.

The origin of the Sandia Mountains as a tilted chunk of the earth's crust is starkly apparent from the east. The plains appear suddenly upended as the relatively flat top of the block slopes up gently to the west, while its exposed edge, just visible from Moriarty, drops precipitously to the basin of the Rio Grande Valley. This range represents just one of the hundreds of tilted fault blocks and alternating valleys comprised by the Basin and Range province, the

Cline's Corners, ca. 1937.

narrowest of the three geographic provinces traversed by Route 66 in New Mexico. Transecting New Mexico's Basin and Range required passing over only one range—the Sandias—and crossing in and out of two basins—the Rio Grande and Puerco valleys—but physical obstacles on this segment compelled road builders to construct the longest diversion from an east-west course anywhere on Route 66. For the first eleven years of the road's existence, Route 66 looped far to the north through Glorieta Pass east of Santa Fe. In 1937 the blading of a road from Santa Rosa to Moriarty and the penetration of the Sandias through the narrow gap of **Tijeras Canyon** allowed for a straighter alignment from east to west. From Moriarty the road began a steady climb up to Sedillo Hill, which at just over 7,000 feet in elevation was the second highest point on Route 66 in New Mexico. From here the road dropped down through the canyon.

For countless generations prehistoric cultures of the valley and those of the plains knew of the opening in the mountains at Tijeras Canyon, formed by a deep fracture in the bedrock. Trade between the Rio Grande Valley and the Great Plains was a keystone of their survival. Corn and other crops from the valley were exchanged for a great source of protein on the hoof—the then-abundant bison herds on the plains. Numerous other trade items, from seashells to turquoise to the feathers of tropical birds, also passed through this and other mountain passes in a far-reaching reticulation of foot trails linking cultures across the Southwest.

At the time of European contact, formidable towns such as Pecos and Taos mediated trade through mountain passes and grew fat on the earnings. At Tijeras Canyon, a few small pueblos may have been standing when the Spanish arrived, but the formerly dominant trade town, Tijeras Pueblo, had

been abandoned. To the south, on the east side of the Manzano Mountains, however, nine separate Tompiro Pueblos thrived, growing crops while also tapping into trade routes through Abo Pass south of the Manzano Mountains.

Postcard of Route 66 as a four-lane highway through Tijeras Canyon, ca. 1951.

Trading patterns begun in prehistoric times continued into the Spanish Colonial era, as courageous traders and hunters made the journey from the sheltered Rio Grande Valley to the wide-open plains and back through Tijeras Canyon, then known as Cañon de Carnue—a name probably derived from the name given by the Tiwa speakers of the Rio Grande Valley for a prehistoric village nearby. Hispanic settlers founded several small plaza towns in the canyon beginning in the late eighteenth century, including Carnuel, San Miguel de Laredo, San Antonio de Padua, and Tijeras, situated near the site of the old Tijeras Pueblo. These settlements held precarious sway, for the long-used trails through the canyon also proved to be a convenient access way for Apache Indians riding west to raid the vulnerable Spanish settlements on the Rio Grande.

With the subjugation of the Apaches and increasing security of the late nineteenth century, farmers began to settle the broad Estancia Valley east of the Sandia Mountains, long since deserted by the Tompiro people. Farmers grew pinto beans there and until the 1930s hauled their crops to Albuquerque on a rough wagon road through the fault at Tijeras—the trace that was the forerunner of the realigned Route 66 and, later, Interstate 40. Rainfall proved fickle and the Estancia Valley bean farmers joined in the massive exodus from the farms of the Southern Plains during the Dust Bowl era.

In **Moriarty**, "the pinto bean capital of the world," the architecture of roadside businesses foreshadowed dramatic cultural changes to come over the mountains. Western, ranch-style design elements and names with references to cowboy culture predominate on Route 66-oriented businesses: the High Valley Café, the Sands Motel, the Lariat Motel, and the Lazy J. But amid these the elements of Southwest Vernacular style become apparent, as some buildings have curved parapets, vigas, and bear Spanish-sounding names. Many of the old Route 66 buildings remain in good form in Moriarty, including the last Whiting Brothers gas station still in operation along Route 66's entire length from Chicago to L.A. Now doing business as Sal's Service Station, the building is typical of the late 1940s gas stations that lined the highway and still shows off its 1960s-vintage neon sign. Unlike tourist courts, which almost ubiquitously utilize Southwest Vernacular or Pueblo Revival elements, gas stations along Route 66 rarely deviate from the national design norms of the day.

El Comedor de Anayas Restaurant, Moriarty.

Four miles past Tijeras, Route 66 begins to exit from the confines of the canyon, opening up the view to the west dramatically. The Mountain Lodge, marked by a sign showing a happy-looking Mexican *paisano* on a burro, stands at this gateway. From this point on, the descent becomes more gradual as Route 66 glides down the *bajada*, or sloping alluvial fan, at the base of the Sandia Mountains and into the long, deep trough of the Rio Grande Rift Valley—a steady drop that totals over 2,000 feet in twelve miles by the time the road bridges the Rio Grande. Mount Taylor, far to the west, comes into view above the verdant floodplain of the Rio Grande and the broad expanse of the West Mesa.

<table>
<tr><td>

ALBUQUERQUE'S
EAST CENTRAL:
THE KING OF
ROUTE 66 STRIPS

</td><td>

The westward-tilted bajada is now cloaked by the sprawling metropolis of Albuquerque, New Mexico's largest city and home to one-third of the state's population, but in 1937 the city of Albuquerque counted only about 35,000 residents in its population and most of the town still huddled close to the old plaza and the rail yards. The creeping sprawl that would characterize the remainder of the century had barely

</td></tr>
</table>

begun, and heavily grazed grasslands dominated the distance between Tijeras and the outskirts of Albuquerque. Albuquerque's famed Central Avenue business strip had just started to stretch east and west as businessmen anticipated the realignment of Route 66 that would bring all of westward-yearning America down Main Street. In 1935, there were only three tourist camps on Central Avenue, while sixteen were strung out along Route 66's old north-south alignment on Fourth Street, parallel to the railroad tracks. The realignment shifted the growth pattern to an east-west direction and broke up the typical railroad-town pattern. By 1941, four years after the realignment, the number of tourist camps on the newly designated Route 66 had grown to thirty-seven and continued to climb to a high of ninety-eight in 1955, when the impending construction of Interstate 40 began to shift the focus of development away from the old axis and out to the freeway. About forty pre-1955 motels remain on Route 66.

Two and a half miles from Central Avenue's eastern terminus at Tramway Boulevard, the **La Puerta Lodge**, built in 1949, presented westward-traveling motorists with one of the first auto court-style motels on the strip. "Puerta" means doorway or passage, and the sign in front of the motel plays on the entranceway theme: its large concrete pillars resemble the columns of a gateway and frame the motel's name, lettered in multicolored neon that at one

La Puerta Lodge, built in 1949, presented westward-traveling motorists with one of the first auto court–style motels on the strip. This Pueblo Revival accommodation, with ornately carved beams, corbels, and posts, continues to serve travelers.
Photographed in 1949.

time flashed synchronously to create an illusion of movement. The sign and original neon remain, although the lights no longer flash, and the motel represents a rare example of a tourist court from Albuquerque's golden days of tourism on Route 66.

The owners of La Puerta carried the doorway theme over into the building design, as each of the court's eight units has an elaborately carved, wooden door with a small, diamond-shaped window. (Initials at the bottom of the original office door, now room one, identify the craftsman who carved the motels doors—A. Ramos.) In keeping with the popular Southwest Vernacular style of their day, the three one-story buildings around the court—the office, the manager's residence, and the motel rooms—are flat-roofed and have white stucco walls with parapets, outlined in neon on the office. A continuous, neon-highlighted portal fronts the motel room block, supported by carved beams and wood posts topped by small corbels. Wood posts likewise frame the garages interspersed between the court's living units.

West of La Puerta, interspersed with contemporary and modern businesses of every stripe, more motels from the 1940s line Route 66. Just down the street there's the Luna Lodge, the Budget 8 Inn (originally the Lo-La-Mi Court) and the Piñon Lodge, the Bow and Arrow (originally the Urban Motor Lodge), the Route 66 Inn (originally the El Jardín Lodge and Café), and many others. Most of the old motels, gas stations, and other Route 66-oriented buildings bear similar clues to their origins: aged, pictorial neon signs, nearly ubiquitous rounded, adobe-like walls, white or brown stucco, and a court-like layout.

The first series of motels that began at La Puerta is interrupted on the north side of the street in one and a half miles by the State Fair Grounds, which occupy some 200 acres. Here Works Progress Administration (WPA) funding allowed the state to construct buildings that offer a more refined expression of southwestern architecture than the stylistic gimmicks of the motels. Buildings at the State Fair Grounds dating from this era include race-horse stables; a racetrack, jockey club, and grandstand; an industrial exhibit building; a poultry building; horse and cattle barns; gates; and the Fine Arts and Indian buildings. The fair's Agriculture Building is one of the earliest structures of this period and is also the most detailed and least altered in form.

Construction of the Agriculture Building would have been impossible without an outpouring of local enthusiasm and funding, orchestrated by the newly appointed State Fair Commission, to supplement WPA funds and labor. The building was constructed between 1936 and 1938 in anticipation of the State Fair's re-opening in October 1938, after a lapse of twenty-two years. It presents an excellent example of the Pueblo Revival style that was so popular with WPA building designers throughout New Mexico. The one-story, flat-roofed building was constructed of adobe bricks made on site by more than one hundred local laborers. It was laid out in a C-shape, with two long wings embracing a large courtyard. Open portals, complete with functional vigas supported by log posts and topped with carved corbels, face the courtyard on each wing. Inside the long wings, two rows of ceiling vigas seventeen feet long were required to span the thirty-foot-wide ceiling. The stout vigas, all 12-18 inches in diameter, support tongue-and-groove *latillas*. A continuous beam 143 feet long, supported by a row of corbelled posts running down the length of each wing, holds up the vigas. Territorial style pediments over the exterior of many of the windows and rope-carved lintels over others, along with rounded parapets, provide additional Pueblo Revival and Territorial style touches.

A half-mile west of the State Fair Grounds, as the business strip picks up again and leads on toward the heart of town, the **Tewa Lodge** presents another outstanding example of a post-World War II tourist court. The name

Neon lighting highlights the upper walls of the Tewa Lodge's Pueblo Revival architecture, and the motel's neon sign—an example of the ubiquitous neon signage that lit up the strip in previous years—hangs out over the sidewalk. Built in 1946, it represents an outstanding example of a largely unaltered, post–World War II tourist court.
Photographed in 1992.

for the motel was taken from a group of closely related Native American Pueblos to the north of Santa Fe. Several other hotels built later in the vicinity also used regional Indian names. All profited from the surge in visitors coming to the State Fair each fall.

The Tewa Lodge is organized in a linear plan of two parallel, single-story wings with parking between them and outside the east wing. Most of the garages interspersed with the rooms have been infilled to create new rooms. A two-story block on the south end of the east wing houses the manager's quarters above and the motel office below. Both buildings have flat roofs, yellow stucco walls, and incorporate several Pueblo Revival style details, including slightly rounded parapets, irregular massing of the second-story portion, battered walls at the office, vigas (appearing at both the office and as supports for entry hoods of many living units), and post-and-corbel framing of some of the garages. Large thunderbird motifs—an image used widely in the Southwest but derived originally from Indian designs in the Great Plains area—decorate the south façade of the office. Neon lighting highlights the upper walls, and the motel's neon sign—one of the best examples of the ubiquitous neon signage that lit up the strip in the 1940s and '50s—hangs out over the sidewalk, held up by a steel post.

Westbound Route 66 continues downhill from the Tewa Lodge, breezing past the slightly newer (mid-1950s) Trade Winds and Desert Sands Motor motels. On the north side of the street, the Zia Lodge (built in 1940) offers another example of an old auto court, with the original plan of motel room/garage/motel room symmetry nearly perfectly preserved. The frame stucco rooms of the Zia incorporated modest details of Pueblo Revival architecture, including small, clay-tiled hoods over each room entrance, flat roofs, and post-and-corbel supports for the garages. The overhead canopy at the office represents a more recent addition to the building, as does the tall neon sign with the Zia sun symbol logo.

> **UPSCALE AND MODERNE TO DOWN HOME AND TRADITIONAL: NOB HILL TO THE UNIVERSITY**

The **Hiland Theater and Shopping Center** on the south side of the road just east of the Zia Lodge was developed in 1952, close on the heels of the 1947 **Nob Hill Business Center**, less than a mile to the west. These fashionable new centers responded to the needs of residents in the budding suburbs of Albuquerque, which was bursting at the seams as it rode a wave of post-WWII growth spurred by newly arrived defense industries. The Nob Hill Business Center is located at the intersection of Central and Carlisle Boulevard, the primary street leading to Kirtland Air Force Base, one of the engines of growth in the 1940s and '50s.

Development in the Nob Hill area began as an extension of the University Heights addition, platted in 1916, but growth was minimal until after World War II. One of the subdivision's developers, one-time mayor Colonel D.K.B. Sellers, co-opted the name "Nob Hill" because, in what seems like a far-reaching stretch of the imagination, the steep incline of Carlisle Boulevard at Central reminded him of the Nob Hill neighborhood in distant San Francisco. As a forward-looking developer with an eye toward marketing, he also hoped that the name would give the new neighborhood the same aristocratic, upscale image associated with the San Francisco district.

The Nob Hill Business Center was Albuquerque's—and New Mexico's—first drive-in shopping center and is one of the best-preserved examples of this phenomenon. As with all shopping centers, the intent of the center was to provide, in one architecturally unified building, spaces for separately owned businesses with an integral, on-site parking area. The development of the Nob Hill Center signaled the business community's first major step in the abandonment of the downtown area. Its construction presaged the vast spread of shopping centers and office complexes that characterizes the setting of Albuquerque and other cities today.

The Hiland Theater and Shopping Center were developed in 1952 following the 1947 Nob Hill Business Center. These fashionable new centers responded to the needs of residents in the budding suburbs of Albuquerque.
Photographed in 1950.

The Nob Hill Business Center occupies three sides of a city block, with the parking lot in the interior space opening onto Central Avenue. Originally, it was designed for twenty-three separate business spaces. A projecting parapet cap, brick courses, and bands of brown tile enhance its strongly horizontal plan. Two angular stepped towers suggestive of the Art Deco style surmount the building's inner corners, while shorter octagonal cupolas top the building's street-side corners. The building steps up in three levels to match the rise of

The Nob Hill Business Center was the most architecturally distinguished building of its day, featuring Streamline Moderne style lines and massing. Albuquerque's first shopping center was designed to communicate the community's wholehearted embrace of change and the promise of the future.
Photograph by Don Usner, 2001.

the hill that it was named after. The business center appears very modest in size today, but in the late 1940s it was by far the most ambitious private building project of its time and the largest commercial construction project in Albuquerque since the completion of the Hilton Hotel (now the La Posada de Albuquerque, on Second Street) in 1938.

The Nob Hill Center was also the most architecturally distinguished building of its day. While contemporary business buildings were generally boxy, utilitarian structures, the Nob Hill center's architect, Louis G. Hesselden, employed modernistic, rounded outside corners, showed off modern building materials, and emphasized horizontal lines—design elements in line with the then-popular national style known as Streamline Moderne. The center is an unusual, relatively unaltered example of this style in Albuquerque. By using Streamline Moderne elements, Hesselden signaled his and much of the community's wholehearted embrace of change and the promise of the future, in contrast to the celebration of the past and tradition evinced by traditional southwestern designs in so many other buildings. Such an approach was consistent with the upscale connotation of the center's name and its location in Albuquerque's newest and fastest growing suburb.

The Jones Motor Company, a few blocks west of the Nob Hill center, also shows the Streamline Moderne style. Not surprisingly, this modern-looking establishment was the brainchild of another forward-looking developer— Route 66 promoter and one-time mayor Ralph Jones. He located this former

This 1949 photograph of the Jones Motor Company illustrates the sleek Streamline Moderne style of this Central Avenue landmark, now operating as a brew pub.

gas station and car dealership on a street corner, thus permitting access from either street to the two gas pumps in front. The most notable Streamline Moderne detail on this one-story, white stucco building is the stepped tower located above its central portion, which once housed the service station's restrooms. Two obliquely facing walls flank the tower, broken by the entries to rooms that once were service bays. The curved walls of the largest parts of the building extend outward from these central elements, giving the building the characteristic Streamline look of the style.

Upon its completion in 1939, the Jones Motor Company became a landmark along the Central Avenue strip, catering both to motorists on Route 66 and residents of the early eastern suburbs of Albuquerque. The gas station was one of the first encountered in Albuquerque by wayfarers traveling west. It opened its doors for business during the Dust Bowl flight of busted farmers from the Southern Plains. The steady stream of "Okies" included many whose overloaded vehicles needed repairs, and often these tottered into town and pulled up at the first gas station on the strip—the Jones Motor Company—seeking repairs. Voluminous, awkward loads hindered access to the working parts of the vehicles, so Jones built a long carport along the southern wall of the garage so that they might unload their vehicles in the shade before he worked on them.

Across the street from the Jones Motor Company, the **Monte Vista Fire Station Number 3** also stood out as a landmark in Albuquerque's blossoming eastern suburbs, but its distinction derived from totally different styling. The

The Monte Vista Fire Station Number 3, built in 1936 with Works Progress Administration funding, is unique among fire stations for its Pueblo Revival style. The city sold the building in 1972 because it could not house newer and wider fire trucks. Photo by Myron Robart, 1950.

fire station owed its construction in 1936 to the availability of WPA funding, and, like most WPA projects in the state, the building incorporated regional architectural styles. Albuquerque's city architect Ernest H. Blumenthal, formerly an employee in the influential Trost and Trost firm that was responsible for many large-scale building projects in the Southwest, drew up plans for the Pueblo Revival-style fire station. It was built, in keeping with all WPA projects, by local labor with local materials. The floor plan devised a two-story rectangle of hollow, stucco-covered block with a three-story hose-drying and stair tower projecting from its southeast corner and a one-story entrance/office projecting from the southwest corner. A one-story addition attached to the rear was added later.

The fire station is small in size but its distinctive design places it on a par with other, much larger examples of local Depression-era buildings of Pueblo Revival style, such as the Agriculture Building at the State Fair Grounds, the Heights Community Center, and the Albuquerque Airport (which Blumenthal also designed). The building's irregular masses, which step up and away from the corner, evoke the communal dwellings of New Mexico's pueblos, while the large double doors, topped by a row of windows, were intended to resemble an entry of a typical Franciscan mission church in New Mexico. The projecting office and tower suggest a two-tower church façade, with one tower left unfinished—not an uncommon occurrence in Spanish Colonial churches. Other Pueblo Revival details include exposed lintels, projecting vigas, and rounded, projecting parapets fronting the flat roofs. The decorative wooden roof ladders were meant to mimic the functional ladders that provided access to dwellings in multistory Native American pueblos.

The Monte Vista Fire Station, carefully restored, now houses a popular restaurant serving a local clientele. Many of its patrons come from the University of New Mexico—the state's largest and oldest college—which lies a few blocks farther west on Route 66. Like the fire station, numerous structures on the university campus exalted traditional styles. The first building on the UNM campus, Hodgin Hall, was completed in 1892 on the east side of Central well beyond the limits of town and just west of the future Nob Hill area. The 1908 remodel of the hall set the tone for future construction at UNM, culminating with the raising of three classic Pueblo Revival buildings—the Student Union, the Administration Building, and Zimmerman Library—in the 1930s. John Gaw Meem, an innovator of the Pueblo Revival style and one of its most prolific proponents, designed all three of these WPA-financed buildings.

PUEBLO-SPANISH TO GOTHIC: OLD MAIN LIBRARY AND ALBUQUERQUE'S FIRST HIGH SCHOOL

Albuquerque's old **main library** on the north side of Route 66 several blocks west of Interstate 40 represents an earlier expression of the Pueblo Revival style and is the one of the finest examples of early Pueblo Revival in the state. The bricks for the library's massive exterior walls were salvaged from the demolition of Albuquerque's first public school, which was built at the site in 1890. The exterior brown stucco emulates the mud used on Pueblo and Spanish Colonial structures. A large portal, supported by carved wood beams and giant vertical posts made of ponderosa pine and large vigas, leads to the main entrance. Carved wood pillars frame the entrance to a small building at the south end of the portal, while the library's main entrance is framed by elaborately carved wood corbels. Low towers on the left and right interrupt the curvilinear parapets of the front facade, and a large bell hangs in an adobe belfry in the middle of the roofline.

The interior of the original building is the most interesting interior space in the total complex. Eight large wood columns support the exposed heavy timber roof construction of darkly stained pine girders and joists, assembled with impressive craftsmanship. The two fireplaces in the main room contain excellent ironwork. A 1978 restoration of the building brought life back to many of the murals, which had been covered over by many layers of paint.

Albuquerque's old main library was built in three phases. The original structure, designed and built by Arthur Rossiter in 1925, is an excellent and rare example of the formative period of Pueblo Revival style architecture. In keeping with the style, architect Gordon Ferguson designed the second phase in 1947 and, with Donald P. Stevens, planned the third phase of construction in 1950.

Just west of the library stands the old **Albuquerque High School**, one of the city's most visible monuments, historically important as the city's first public high school and as a part of the historic district in which it stands. Now vacant and boarded, this was Albuquerque's only high school from 1914 to 1948, and it continued in use into the 1970s. (The City of Albuquerque obtained title to six of the seven school buildings in 1996 and has an agree-

As the city's first public high school, Albuquerque High is one of the most visible monuments in the Huning Highlands Historic District. The architectural firm of Trost and Trost designed the first building of the complex in 1914 in Collegiate Gothic Revival style with elements of the Dutch Revival. As city growth continued, the high school added additional buildings over time. Now boarded up and awaiting reincarnation as loft apartments, offices, and businesses, this important site will continue to yield fond memories for its alumni.
Photographed in 1946.

ment with a local developer to transform classrooms into loft apartments and other spaces into high-tech, office, or business use.)

The Albuquerque School Board first considered a proposal to build a high school in 1893 but it took another twenty-one years for plans and money to come together in the form of the building, designed by the prestigious architectural firm of Trost and Trost. The initial classroom, Old Main, consisted of one large building that could house 500 students. The plan incorporated the latest innovations in school design, including a science laboratory, gymnasium, and 850-seat auditorium. It was furnished with the most up-to-date equipment—steel lockers, business machines, typewriters, and a completely furnished kitchen for home economics classes. Facing Central Avenue and long a landmark, Old Main's design corresponds to the Collegiate Gothic style that was prevalent in late-nineteenth- and early-twentieth-century school buildings. The style is characterized by masonry construction with brick cornices and white trim and large, multi-pane windows on all elevations. The pedimented roofline, cast-stone trim coping, repetitive dormer windows in the towers, and belt course add elements of the formal Dutch Revival style.

Starting in 1927, four structures were added to the high school over the next two decades to form a complex of buildings closely related in design and clustered around a central courtyard: the Manual Arts Building, designed by George Williamson, followed by the Classroom Building, Gymnasium Building, and Library Building, all three designed by Louis G. Hesselden (architect of the Nob Hill Business Center) and built with manpower organized and paid for by the WPA.

CLASSY SKYSCRAPERS AND DECO-MADE PUEBLO: ALBUQUERQUE'S OLD NEW TOWN BY THE TRACKS

The high school lies within the gridwork of streets that defined the limits of the original townsite of New Albuquerque, platted in 1885. New Town had begun as a shipping point on the new Atlantic and Pacific Railroad in 1880 when Albuquerque's population numbered 2,325. Its designation as a major maintenance center on the Atchison, Topeka, and Santa Fe Railway fueled rapid growth, and Albuquerque soon boasted the largest rail yards west of the Mississippi. The realigned Route 66 followed this, the main road and only oil-surfaced thoroughfare through the heart of New Town. It was a street much like others in railroad towns in the West, with two- and three-story brick buildings clustered near the old railroad depot. Railroad Avenue, as it was known until 1907 when it was renamed Central, was equipped with streetcars that carried passengers back and forth between the railroad-oriented business district and the

The Sunshine Building:
Henry Trost built this
Beaux Arts Commercial
edifice in 1924.
Photograph ca. 1930.

old Spanish Colonial plaza one mile to the west, called Old Town.

Just west of the high school Central Avenue slips under the railroad tracks, which define the downtown district's eastern margin. Here travelers in the 1920s through the '50s encountered Albuquerque's original skyscrapers, the **Sunshine Building** and the First National Bank Building, which remain on the block as impressive monuments. The two buildings rose up within a block of each other among their humbler neighbors in the bustling downtown area. They still convey a stately grandeur reminiscent of the prosperous, pre-depression years in which they were built.

The Sunshine Building's six-story height makes it substantial but not out of scale with the smaller buildings nearby. It is easy to take in the full height of the building while standing on the street, but the building's design and ornamentation contribute to its stature as much as its size. Using terms that could apply to a sculpture, architectural historian Edna Bergman has summarily described the Sunshine Building as "graceful, dignified, and well proportioned." From a historical perspective, the building reflects the prevailing mood in Albuquerque in the promising 1920s, when the flourishing town had a sense of itself as a prosperous and ambitious city. Many leading business-people maintained offices in the building, and the theater on the ground level on the north side of the building was a center of the downtown entertainment scene for decades. In renovated form, it is again a popular theater.

In building style, the Sunshine Building is usually described as Beaux Arts Commercial. Its designer, Henry Trost, distinguished himself with many building projects in the Southwest, including major buildings in almost every town in New Mexico and six in Albuquerque that have earned a place on the National Register of Historic Places. Some credit Trost with greater influence on southwestern architecture than John Gaw Meem.

The upper five stories of the Sunshine are faced with variegated, buff-colored brick and ornaments of cast stone, while smooth stone finishes the ground level. The building's west and north sides show expressive but restrained ornamentation. On both sides, the ground floor facing is topped with a simple molded stringcourse, giving the building a well-defined base. The west side, dominated by horizontal, symmetrical rows of double-hung wood windows and widely spaced cast stone ornaments on its left and right edges, bears the least additional ornamentation. On the north face, raised rectangular columns with capitals and bases and a central group of panels above the two-story theater entrance lend a strong vertical emphasis. The top floor is marked off by more cast-stone stringcourses and by a row of ornamented panels above the windows, also made of cast stone. The panels are capped with a deeply indented cornice and a parapet pierced with a cast-stone balustrade and ornamented with more cast-stone panels. Corbel brackets support an ornamental balcony across the north-side theater entrance,

which was originally sheltered by a glass canopy. The theater, originally gilded and decorated, was designed to accommodate both cinema and stage performances and seated 920 in orchestra and balcony.

Just a half-block north of the Sunshine Building stands the **old Hilton Hotel**, another one of the downtown district's most elegant historic buildings and the only survivor of Albuquerque's three great

The Franciscan Hotel was designed in 1923 by Henry Charles Trost in Pueblo Revival style. During downtown Albuquerque's urban renewal efforts, the hotel was demolished in 1972. Photographed ca. 1930.

La Posada de Albuquerque, formerly the Hilton Hotel, was the first modern high-rise hotel in the city. Designed by Anton F. Korn and opened in 1939, the building represents a unique blending of commercial architecture and traditional southwestern design in the Territorial Revival style. Like the Alvarado and Franciscan hotels, its original plan and furnishings were rooted in New Mexico artistic traditions. The hotel interior retains its original southwestern flavor. Photograph by Don Usner, 2001.

"southwestern" hotels. Like the **Alvarado Hotel** and the Franciscan Hotel, the interior design and furnishings of the old Hilton Hotel were rooted in New Mexican arts and crafts, and, also like the others, the Hilton was designed and completed by artists who immersed themselves in local design traditions. The Alvarado was demolished in 1970 and the Franciscan Hotel in 1972, but the Hilton maintains its architectural form and interior detailing in its current incarnation as **La Posada de Albuquerque**.

This was not the hotel that the average traveler on Route 66 sought out for lodging. When the Hilton was opened in 1939 it was the first modern, high-rise hotel in Albuquerque, then a small western town of 50,000 residents. During the following decade, Albuquerque experienced explosive growth, and the Hilton became the center of the city's political and social life as well as the place of lodging for many of its most distinguished visitors, from politicians to movie stars to nuclear scientists. The hotel offered the only modern ballroom and meeting facilities in the city, and a group of leading politicians, businessmen, and government officials made the hotel—and, more commonly, the bar and lobby—their unofficial club.

The hotel was designed by Anton F. Korn, a Texan who designed Hilton hotels in Lubbock and El Paso before moving to Taos and becoming interested in southwestern styling. In the Albuquerque Hilton, he blended modernism and traditional southwestern styling in a manner suitable for a city in transition. The formal, modern exterior suggests a functionalism related more closely to the commercial architecture of eastern cities than to the Pueblo Revival style that was so popular among southwestern architects of the day. On the exterior of the hotel's two distinct blocks—an eight-story residential block and a wider, two-story section for public rooms—southwestern styling is apparent only in the white stucco walls and the wide, decorative brick corbel courses at each roof line, which relate to the Territorial Revival style. The clean, symmetrical forms and straight lines of the structure offer no hint of the Southwestern refinement inside.

The Alvarado complex of gift shops, hotel, restaurant, railroad depot, and offices was designed by Charles F. Whittlesey in 1901 and opened the following year. The first Mission Revival style development in the city, it featured towers, parapets, tiled roofs, secluded courtyards, and wood-beamed ceilings. This impressive complex served as a Fred Harvey establishment until its demolition in 1970. A new transportation depot, reminiscent of the original complex, now occupies the site.

Two hallways, decorated with pictorial murals—among the few survivors of the numerous murals that decorated the walls of the original hotel, many painted by local artists—lead into the interior of the hotel from south and east entrances. One mural depicts tourist attractions of New Mexico and the other New Mexican settlers. The hallways open to the large, two-story lobby, amply apportioned with carved wood and southwestern accents—clearly the high point of the hotel's architectural statement.

Rounded arches elaborately decorated with wood wainscoting define the north and south sides of the lobby, while pairs of corbel-capped wood posts demarcate its east and west margins. The posts on the east frame the hotel's east entrance, while the pair on the west, which used to lead to the elevator access, now flank a large bar of rich wood backed by a mirror. Square decorated vigas, supported by richly carved wood corbels with flat board *latillas* laid between them, hold up the lobby's lofty, second-story ceiling. Carved wood surrounds the elevator openings and embellishes the ceilings of the first-floor corridors. An open mezzanine on the second floor overlooks the lobby, its large, square, plastered columns suggesting a continuation of the lines of the first-floor arch pillars. A carved wood railing connects the pillars on all four sides of the mezzanine.

The furnishings of the original Hilton included light fixtures designed and made by Walter Gilbert, who created the ironwork in the KiMo Theater, furniture constructed from hand-carved wood and leather, and specially woven carpets utilizing Native American patterns. Many of these were lost in renovations of the Hilton, but the current owner of La Posada de Albuquerque, who bought the severely neglected hotel in 1982, restored it to its original craftsmanship. He also has endeavored to recover or remake lost items so that the lobby once again is filled with handmade southwestern furniture, returning the hotel to its former opulence.

The **KiMo Theater** on Central Avenue three blocks west of the Sunshine Building is another of downtown Albuquerque's most architecturally significant buildings. When it was built in 1926-27, it couldn't compete in size with the new skyscrapers in town. Instead it achieved prominence through use of extravagant and elaborate detailing, inside and out. Arguably the most ornate theater ever built in New Mexico, the KiMo dates to a period when movie madness was sweeping the country and designing movie theaters became a unique specialty. The "movie palaces" from this era represent some of the "richest and most extravagantly romantic architecture this country has ever produced," in the words of architecture critic Ada Louise Huxtable. The KiMo Theater is an extraordinary regional expression of this American architectural phenomenon.

Recently renovated to its former glory, the KiMo Theater was designed by Carl Boller in 1926 and shows strong Art Deco influences. Native American elements used to embellish the structure set the KiMo apart, resulting in a regional style of architecture known as "Pueblo Deco." Photographed ca. 1929.

Albuquerque businessman and theater owner Oreste Bachechi went to Hollywood to find an architect for the new movie palace he envisioned for Central Avenue, and there he met Carl Boller, senior partner in a firm renowned for its theater designs throughout the West. Boller traveled all over New Mexico visiting pueblos and reservations and gathering design material. Pablo Abeita, the progressive and influential governor of Albuquerque's nearest Native American neighbor, Isleta Pueblo, won a $50 reward when he suggested KiMo as the winning name for the theater. In Abeita's native Tiwa language the word meant "king of its kind" and referred to the mountain lion, a revered animal and important figure in the Pueblo pantheon.

For his KiMo Theater, Boller utilized a basic floor plan common to many of his theater designs, with an overall design scheme strongly influenced by the then-popular Art Deco movement. What set the KiMo apart were the Native American elements used to ornament and embellish the structure. The resulting romanticized regional style of architecture was later dubbed "Pueblo Deco," unique to the Southwest. The Art Deco influence shows up in the strong verticality of the front façade, enhanced by linear elements, bright colors, and geometric motifs. Native American symbols dominate the relief ornamentation on the south and west facades and throughout the theater's lavishly decorated interior. Bachechi spared no expense in creating a theater that would capture the imagination of a generation during a heady time. He was not disappointed when more than 2,000 people attended the 1927 gala opening night, including Albuquerque's mayor, the state's U.S. senator and a former governor, and Pueblo leaders from Tesuque, Cochití, and Isleta. To reiterate the Indian theme of the décor, the program featured sixty Native dancers and singers along with the screening of a new Hollywood film.

The KiMo fell into disuse with the decline of downtown on the heels of the 1960s exodus to the suburbs. It suffered a fire in the 1970s that destroyed the proscenium and stage area. The city of Albuquerque purchased the building in 1977 and completed a meticulous renovation in 2000 that utilized historic photos to restore the theater with careful attention to its rich ornamentation.

The KiMo stands a modest three stories high (its fly loft reaches five stories) and is made of brick, like all the neighboring buildings on the block. The exterior bricks are visible only on the north side of the building, facing the alley; elsewhere they are finished with strongly textured, light-brown stucco ornamented with details of glazed, terra-cotta tile. Vividly colored relief work decorates the surface, the dominant feature consisting of rows of circular shields adorned with pendants above the second-story windows. The original marquee made of iron has been replaced with the theater's large, vertical electric sign, which projected out from the marquee.

In the 1920s few substantial buildings in Albuquerque failed to incorporate Indian motifs in their design or décor but none did so so extravagantly as the KiMo. From kachina figures on lamp shades to lightning bolts on the ceiling, the KiMo is a rich and colorful mélange of design motifs loosely adapted from Indian cultures of the Southwest. "Indian" motifs dominate the geometric lines as well as the shields of the KiMo Theater's facades and continue to the interior. They adorn the ceiling and vigas in the entrance vestibule, where the lighting fixture represents the so-called Farewell Canoe—a mythological canoe towed by an eagle that was supposed to have carried a dead Indian warrior. In the two-story theater lobby, chandeliers hang between vigas decorated by vividly painted symbols of Indian origin. The room's five square support columns are detailed with plaster-of-Paris ornamentation and topped with lighting sconces fashioned of skulls from longhorn cattle—not an Indian motif, but a popular icon of the Southwest nonetheless. Stairways on both sides of the lobby lead to an open mezzanine. Murals, visible from the mezzanine, adorn all four upper walls of the lobby. The scenes, painted by German-born artist Carl von Hassler, depict the Seven Cities of Cíbola—the legendary place of limitless wealth that initially motivated Spanish explorers to penetrate deep into the Southwest in the sixteenth century. The outlines of Indian-styled birds repeat themselves in patterns in the wrought-iron railings—the work of Walter Gilbert—on the stairs and mezzanine.

Remarkably, all the apparent woodwork in the KiMo is made not of wood but of plaster. The builders carefully inscribed grain-line patterns in the plaster and painted them brown to create the illusion of fine, darkly stained pine. Large vigas, painted with figures from Navajo mythology, cross with smaller vigas to span the ceiling of the nearly square auditorium, which seated 850 in the orchestra and 450 in the balcony. Alternate sections between the smaller vigas are decorated with zigzag lightning symbols. Vigas beneath the balcony are also decorated, while the spaces between them are ornamented with zigzag patterns similar to those in the lobby. Like those in the lobby, the auditorium lighting fixtures represent the Farewell Canoe. Ornamental plaster-of-paris reliefs topped by longhorn skull sconces, like those in the lobby, line the theater's sidewalls. A frieze with longhorn skulls and symbols of Indian origin borders the proscenium.

Maisel's Indian Trading Post, located on the south side of Route 66 a half-block west of the KiMo, opened in 1939 and also is replete with Indian designs. John Gaw Meem, a leading architect of the day who left his stamp all over New Mexico, designed the Trading Post, although the building doesn't resemble the Pueblo Revival or Territorial Revival styles for which Meem earned notoriety. Instead, this small building showed influence of the Art Deco style. In the trading post, Meem devised the storefront with large display windows that clearly show off the store's wares. The Black Carrara structural glass at the base of the windows is a typical feature in Art Deco storefronts. A continuous panel painted with a colorful mural depicting southwestern Indians in ceremonial clothing tops the display windows. Pablita Velarde, the acclaimed Santa Clara Pueblo painter, and other well-known

Maisel's Indian Trading Post, completed in 1939, was known for its mural renderings by well-known Indian artists, who were commissioned by architect John Gaw Meem. The Maisel family was one of the first trading families to see the potential of large-scale crafts production and during its heyday employed over 300 craftsmen on the premises. Photographed in 1948.

Navajo and Pueblo artists of the time painted these detailed murals. They are fine examples of the flat-art style of painting that Indian students at the Santa Fe Indian School developed in the 1930s.

The display windows at Maisel's recede at the entry, forming a large, protected space twenty feet deep flanked by additional display windows. The murals continue above these windows, showing more dancers, singers and other figures as well as gracefully rendered animals and a stylized thunderbird-like figure. The terra-cotta flooring in the entryway bears Indian designs and the name "Maisel's" inlaid in silver dollars in front of double wood-framed, commercial doors. Inside, large display cases and counters in the showroom exhibit large quantities of Indian-made goods as well as products of Hispanic artisans from the Southwest. The Maisel family was one of the first trading families to see the potential of large-scale crafts production for both retail and wholesale purposes. The building's basement functioned as an atelier for Indian craftspeople; a wide, open stairway allowed patrons to observe the artisans at work. During its heyday in the late 1940s and early '50s, Maisel employed some 300 craftsmen on the premise, making it the largest store of its kind in the world.

Art Deco styling is more obvious in the **Skinner Building**, erected in 1931 at the corner of Eighth Street and Central Avenue on the western margin of downtown Albuquerque. The building, designed by architect A.W. Boehning—

The Skinner Building, erected in 1931, is one of the very few examples of Art Deco architecture in Albuquerque.

another of the many Albuquerque architects who at one time was employed by the Trost and Trost firm—has been described as a pocket-sized version of the style. It is one of the very few examples of Art Deco architecture in Albuquerque. The building, smooth and simple in concept, is detailed with abundant abstract and geometric details that seem almost extravagant on such a small edifice—especially one originally designed as a grocery store. Its modest size in part reflects the austerity of the early Depression era when it was built.

The Skinner Building served as the main grocery store and office for the J. A. Skinner Stores and Markets from 1931 through 1942 and has since seen many shingles come and go. The building has always been divided into two main stores by a north-south wall. The interior of the east-side store retains the original pressed-metal ceiling, a ceramic tile wainscoting with geometric motifs, and original light fixtures. The west-side store has been remodeled by the addition of a suspended ceiling. Currently, the building houses a restaurant.

The accessible north and west facades of the brick Skinner Building are surfaced in terra-cotta with full-width display windows dominating the main north-facing façade. The handsome pillars at each end of the north façade are marked by stylized papyrus designs framed by spiral ornaments. Several bands of geometric design suggestive of Native American patterning top the display windows. The horizontal geometry continues above in a bronze-covered transom bar that is glazed with small squares of opalescent glass in a green-and-black diamond pattern. Above the transom bar, bands of decorative tiles, one band at the base and two at the cornice, border the terra-cotta façade. Five elegant pillars, slightly narrower than the pair on the north side, divide the west façade of the building into four bays. The pillars repeat the stylized papyrus motif of the front pillars. Details of the north façade are repeated, on a smaller scale, above an entrance door on the south end of the façade.

OUT OF THE
BOSQUE AND UP
THE MESA:
THE WEST CENTRAL
STRIP AND NINE
MILE HILL

The core of old downtown Albuquerque tapers off past the Skinner Building but businesses oriented toward Route 66 continue. In about a mile the road swings by streets leading to the Old Town Plaza, site of the original Spanish Colonial village of Albuquerque, founded in 1706. The buildings around the town square conform to the settlement plan dictated by Spanish law, which intended for frontier towns like Albuquerque to be capable of self-defense. The plaza was primarily a residential compound, with some government buildings and the dominant presence of the church on the northwest corner. The buildings have been modified and rebuilt over the centuries but remain essentially true to their original design. The most significant is the San Felipe de Neri Church, whose simple adobe construction and unsophisticated style match the rustic elegance of many churches in Spanish Colonial villages.

El Vado Court, a few blocks past Old Town on Central Avenue, takes its name from the origins of Albuquerque: *vado* means ford, and Albuquerque began as a small town at a crossing of the Rio Grande. It was one of many small plaza towns along the old supply route to Mexico, the Camino Real, or Royal Road, but had the distinction of being one of only three *villas* in New Mexico under Spanish rule. El Vado Court is situated just upriver from the ford in the river (located where Bridge Street bridge now crosses the river) that was the tiny nucleus from which the metropolis of Albuquerque grew.

The El Vado is an excellent example of a pre-World War II tourist court along Route 66 and is the oldest one along the West Central Avenue com-

The El Vado Court, a classic pre-war tourist court. Built in 1937 in anticipation of the opening of the rerouted Route 66, Pueblo Revival architectural elements and the vintage neon sign still beckon travelers to stay.

mercial strip. It was built in 1937 in anticipation of the opening of the rerouted Route 66. Its two buildings comprise thirty-two units facing a parking courtyard. Garages are interspersed between the units. Gas pumps used to stand in front of the motel office at the north end of the east building, beneath the ornate neon sign that still stands. The sign shows the motel's name in bold letters, with a stylized Indian surrounded by rainbow-colored headdress. Pueblo Revival architectural elements on the building include buttressed walls, curvilinear parapets, irregular massing, and exposed vigas. Exceptionally ornate use of the style appears in the lobby adjoining the office, where exposed vigas supporting a dark wood ceiling, a raised stucco and tile-framed fireplace, and an ornate wrought-iron lighting fixture create a picturesque interior.

El Vado is the last old motel before Route 66 enters the *bosque* (cottonwood woodland) and crosses the Rio Grande. The broad, heavily silted waterway of the Rio Grande blocked travel westward out of Albuquerque until it was bridged in 1931. The bosque was protected from development for centuries by the intransigence of the river, but now the river and its bosque are struggling. Urban development of the floodplain, along with activities upstream—dam building, overgrazing, deforestation, and water withdrawals for urban and agricultural uses—have changed the river flow dramatically, leaving fish populations teetering on the brink of extinction and the cottonwoods without the annual floods they need to reproduce. Despite these problems, however, the bosque along the Rio Grande still has some vigor and is the best riverine ecosystem in the greater Southwest.

After crossing the Rio Grande Route 66 begins a long, slow climb up **Nine Mile Hill**—the ascent of the West Mesa that for eleven years daunted road builders and forced the bypass southward through Los Lunas. The strip continues, lit in the 1950s and '60s by the flashy neon of businesses like the Western View Diner and Steak House, the Cibola Court, the Hilltop Lodge, the Hacienda Motel, El Campo Tourist Court, Siesta Court, La Hacienda Camp, the Westward Ho Motel, and the Dairy Store. Many of these businesses still remain. The strip began to thin out and the neon glow faded by the time Route 66 came to the Last Chance Gas Station and crossed 98th Street to aim for the wide-open spaces where the horizon is broken only by the pointed summits of the West Mesa volcanoes.

The West Mesa seems a minor obstacle today, but its steep, sandy escarpment turned away road builders from the earliest days of wagon travel. Instead of struggling up the mesa, which military road builders in the nineteenth century described as "the worst part of the road to California," the westward-bound travelers turned south here and continued along the Rio Grande to Los Lunas, where a breach in the escarpment and lower grades made the climb easier. Not surprisingly, the Los Lunas route coincided with the throughway chosen by railroad engineers.

West of 98th Street, Route 66 and I-40 run closely parallel and in a few miles crest the West Mesa at the top of Nine Mile Hill, offering spectacular views to the east and west. Travelers going west could look back over their shoulders from this high point, more than 500 feet above the crossing of the Rio Grande, to get a last look at the Rio Grande Valley, including the glittering metropolis of Albuquerque, and its flanking mountain ranges. Westward, the view opens expansively across the broad Rio Puerco Valley to warm-toned mesas of the Colorado Plateau and the nearly 12,000-foot-high summit of Mount Taylor.

The **Rio Puerco**, the second largest drainage basin of the Basin and Range province crossed by Route 66, presented another obstacle to road builders of Route 66. While the Rio Puerco normally carried only a trickle of water, summer rains could trigger massive floods. This area was once a fertile valley, with a flowing stream at its center bordered by cottonwood trees. By the 1930s, as the realigned Route 66 made its way westward, a deep, eroded chasm imprisoned an ephemeral trickle of mud. Small Hispanic towns once drew their sustenance from this watershed, but cycles of devastating erosion left the river entrenched in this wash.

The degraded Rio Puerco presented formidable challenges to those trying to straighten out Route 66 and bring it directly west from Albuquerque. Floods in the river washed out bridge abutments, and the original alignment of Route 66 steered far to the south in part to avoid crossing the Rio Puerco. Route 66 boosters in Albuquerque advocated an alignment to take the road straight west from the city. The first step was complete when the Rio Grande was bridged, but funding for a **bridge on the Puerco** was hard to come by until 1933, when the Roosevelt administration provided emergency federal funds for highway construction. The bridge was completed within a year and many people began using the road, although the Laguna Cutoff didn't officially became part of U.S. 66 until 1937.

To span the tempestuous Rio Puerco, highway engineers used a single-span, Parker Through-Truss bridge—a type of bridge design favored by road builders in the 1920s and '30s. They placed unusually massive bridge abutments on deeply driven pilings to compensate for the eroding river and its unstable river banks, then constructed a single, 250-foot span capable of clearing the entire river floodplain—the longest single-span bridge of its kind in the Southwest. The span consists of ten panels measuring twenty-five feet in length, each with its top chord at a different angle to make the polygonal top chord characteristic of Parker Through-Truss bridges. The striking arch of the superstructure appears in marked relief to the newer, ground-level steel-

beam bridges of I-40 that parallel it. It is one of only a handful of truss bridges left in New Mexico. Along with a portion of old Route 66 that remains to the east, the bridge was part of a frontage road that provided access to roadside businesses at the Rio Puerco. In 2001 a new bridge was placed for frontage road traffic.

Beyond the Rio Puerco, Route 66 fades into obscurity for several miles until it is accessible and in use again just east of Laguna Pueblo, where the pre-1937 alignment comes in from the south to join the new route.

Built in 1933, the Rio Puerco bridge is the longest through-truss bridge in the region and one of a handful left in New Mexico.
Photographed in 1933.

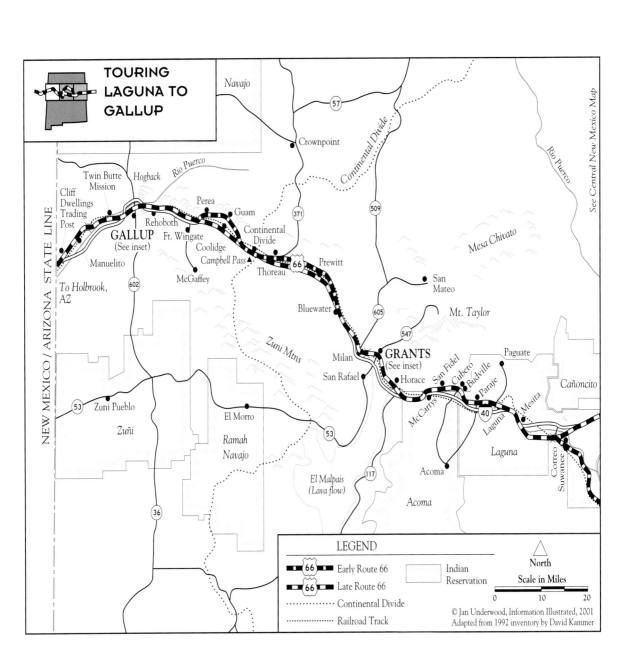

TOURING LAGUNA TO GALLUP

Navajo

57

Crownpoint

Continental Divide

See Central New Mexico Map

Rio Puerco

Rio Puerco

Twin Butte Mission
Hogback
Cliff Dwellings Trading Post
Perea
Guam
371
509
GALLUP (See inset)
Rehoboth
Ft. Wingate
Coolidge
Continental Divide
Mesa Chivato
Manuelito
Campbell Pass
McGaffey
Thoreau
66
Prewitt
San Mateo
NEW MEXICO / ARIZONA STATE LINE
602
To Holbrook, AZ
Bluewater
605
Mt. Taylor
Zuni Mtns
547
Milan
GRANTS (See inset)
San Fidel
Cubero
Paguate
53
Zuni Pueblo
Zuñi
El Morro
San Rafael
Horace
McCartys
Budville
Paraje
Cañoncito
Ramah Navajo
53
Mesita
Laguna
40
Laguna
36
117
El Malpais (Lava flow)
Acoma
Correo
Suwanee
Acoma

© Jan Underwood, Information Illustrated, 2001
Adapted from 1992 inventory by David Kammer

LEGEND

66 Early Route 66

66 Late Route 66

Continental Divide

Railroad Track

Indian Reservation

North

Scale in Miles

0   10   20

TOUR FOUR

TOURING LAGUNA
TO
GALLUP

**THE
HIGH AND DRY
PLATEAU**

Travelers continuing on Highway 66 from Laguna to Gallup, and twenty miles more to the Arizona border, crossed the southern reach of one of the Southwest's most spectacular geographic provinces, the Colorado Plateau. Here, the alternating valleys and mountain ranges of the Basin and Range and the Rio Grande Rift give way to a terrain of layered sandstone lifted over a mile above sea level—a windswept, hard-edged land dominated by scrubby woodlands of piñon and juniper trees. Not only would travelers encounter these new landforms, much more exotic than any encountered before on the route west, they would find themselves entering the domain of new cultural groups. The Navajo people are the most widespread and numerous of the several Native groups that call this, one of the world's largest and highest plateaus, their home, and they become more populous with each mile westward. The pueblos of Laguna, Isleta, and Acoma, as well as numerous Hispanic towns have also made this part of the plateau their home for centuries.

The change from Basin and Range to Colorado Plateau begins as the old route climbs alongside the railroad tracks up the valley of the San José River southwest of Albuquerque to Correo. The cottonwood *bosques* of the Rio

Grande and the oasis-like Hispanic and Indian towns that cling to the river's bank—home to over half of New Mexico's population—fall behind as the expansive view west takes over. Dun-colored mesas recede to a distant horizon, with the azure pyramid of Mount Taylor offering the only vertical relief. Scanning the vast panorama of mesas the eye returns again and again to this graceful summit. It is not possible to traverse this landscape without looking up and wondering what lies on the snowy summit or in the cool forests on its flanks. Like many landmarks in the spacious lands of the West, it beacons for many miles, pulling like a magnet and marking the distance traveled as it grows closer and closer. It's no wonder that all Native groups in the region revere Mount Taylor and ascribe it spiritual and cosmological significance.

LAGUNA:

A

HILLTOP PUEBLO

ON THE PLATEAU

Route 66 travelers probably heard some of the Indian stories about the mountain from traders or local guides at the roadside businesses that clung to the slender ribbon of highway in two clusters between Laguna and McCartys. A rough section of old Route 66 is accessible between Laguna and Correo south of Interstate 40. Much easier access is available at Mesita, an outlying village of Laguna Pueblo.

Mesita stands out among all the surrounding pueblos because its homes are constructed of black basalt from the surrounding mesas rather than of adobe. Laguna tribal members who were disenchanted with the Pueblo leadership founded the village in the 1870s. These conservative defectors included many of the old villages' medicine men, who took their religious implements and moved away rather than tolerating the progressive elements that welcomed Protestant missionaries into the pueblo. Some of the medicine people and their followers continued on to seek shelter at Isleta, where they were welcomed and made homes.

Just a few miles from Mesita, after rounding infamous Dead Man's Curve, Route 66 swings around sandstone mesas and comes to the old village of Laguna on a hill overlooking the San José River Valley. Laguna may be the most photographed of all the pueblos, with the possible exception of Taos, because of its picturesque setting and because an official pullout on the Interstate offers postcard-perfect views of the pueblo. The AT&SF railroad used to curve around the base of the hill before it was relocated a mile to the east, and the nearness of the trains prompted the development of a trade between Lagunas and passengers. Trade with the outside world was also mediated by the local trader, Sigfried Abraham, at his Old Laguna Trading Post, near the tracks at the base of the hill.

The present pueblo of Laguna formed after the Pueblo Revolt of 1680 and the Spanish reconquest of New Mexico twelve years later. Displaced refugees from Keresan-speaking pueblos along the Rio Grande relocated to Laguna, where they joined western Keresans from Acoma. With an official founding date of 1699, Laguna is often called the newest of the pueblos, even though there is evidence that people lived at the site long before the present village was built.

The most prominent feature of Laguna Pueblo when seen from afar is the white-stuccoed Catholic Church, which perches prominently at the apex of the hill above the brown-toned adobes of the pueblo. The church, built in 1699, is an elegant example of mission church architecture; Santa Fe architects emulated its bell towers when they designed the Museum of Fine Arts in Santa Fe. In size, the San José mission can't compare with the San Esteban mission at nearby Acoma Pueblo, which also inspired early versions of the Pueblo Revival style. The Laguna church could fit, in its entirety, inside of the Acoma mission. The real treasure of the Laguna church is to be found inside, in its artwork and especially its altar screen.

The altar screen, or *reredo*, and the religious paintings on animal hide are excellent examples of the religious folk art tradition that developed in Spanish Colonial New Mexico—a tradition that represents a blending of European, Mexican, and local influences. An anonymous Franciscan friar known to the world today as the Laguna Santero painted both the reredo and the hide paintings at the San José mission in the early nineteenth century. This prolific santero (maker of religious art) painted some thirty reredos in New Mexico, including the large one in the San Esteban mission at Acoma, but none is so well preserved as the one at Laguna. The Laguna painting is executed in a simplified Mexican Baroque style that was obsolete in metropolitan Mexico by 1700 but flourished in New Mexico into the eighteenth century. The Laguna Santero mentored the first Native *santeros* in New Mexico at his Santa Fe workshop. These artists in turn spread the tradition throughout New Mexico and southern Colorado.

Besides illustrating the best of indigenous Spanish Colonial artwork, paintings in the Laguna mission also provide a good example of the way that Pueblo artists modified and adapted Catholicism at many of the pueblos. Contrasting with the somber reredos, the canopy over the altar, representing the sun, the moon, and a rainbow against a starlit sky, conveys lightness and celebration of nature. This appears to be the work of a converted Laguna Christian utilizing Native American imagery. Women artists from the pueblo made the paintings along the nave that rhythmically repeat terraces and birds. These images derive from traditional Pueblo pictorial systems in kiva murals and in pottery and symbolically refer to kachinas, rainfall, and fertility. The birds may result from the regular involvement of Parrot Clan women in the periodic repainting of the walls of the church.

Route 66 leaves Laguna along the railroad tracks, heading west toward Mount Taylor and its skirt of dark basalt mesas. It passes through New Laguna, a railroad town within Laguna Pueblo, and the outlying Laguna village of Paraje. On the north side of the road, just below Paraje Mesa, stand the remains of a stone and concrete tourist court complex from the 1940s. The Paraje Trading Post, built of adobe with a brick façade in Southwest Vernacular style, also clings to the north side of the road.

<table>
<tr><td>

**TRADING POSTS
AND
CRUMBLING WALLS:
BUDVILLE TO
MCCARTYS**

</td><td>

Eight miles west of Laguna Pueblo Route 66 veers to aim straight for Mount Taylor and swings into Budville, a strip of largely abandoned roadside businesses along the route. Bud Rice opened a service station and touring business here in 1938 and his namesake, the **Budville Trading Company,** stands on the south side of the road under the branches of

</td></tr>
</table>

leaning Siberian elms. The bold red-and-white sign in front and the tall water tower in back draw every driver's attention to the now closed-up building. Budville bears slight architectural resemblance to nearby Indian pueblos and Hispanic towns and their run-down, ancient cores. Gas pump islands and a broad gravel parking area in front, motel rooms behind, the empty store now is protected by wrought-iron bars bearing clichéd southwestern motifs.

Across the road from the Budville Trading Company, the similarly white-washed Scottie's Trading Post bleaches in the sun along with the withered remains of a few other buildings that form a ghost strip of roadside services. Although the trading posts and other businesses that served Route 66 traffic have dried up, two bars and the LA (Laguna-Acoma) Baptist Church (Truckers Welcome!) seem to be doing well in spite of the fact that there seem to be almost no people living here.

The "LA"—or Laguna-Acoma—designation acknowledges Budville's location near the border between lands belonging to Laguna and Acoma. Drawing tourists by the thousands, Acoma boasts that its mesatop village is the oldest continuously occupied town in America. Archaeologists date it to about A.D. 1000. Acoma is recognized as one of the architectural and historical treasures of the Southwest, and people moving west for pleasure on Route 66 often took in a detour, usually with the guidance of an experienced local like Bud Rice.

Without a map to show that Budville is situated just outside two pueblos where alcoholic beverages cannot be legally sold, it's hard to imagine who would come to the two thriving bars here. The illusion of Budville's isolation from patrons becomes more apparent if you turn right at a road junction beside the bar just up the road from Budville, following the alignment of Route 66 before it was rerouted in 1937. In less than a mile this side road passes a cemetery and leads to the old but still lively community of **Cubero**, probably named after New Mexico's Governor Pedro Rodríguez Cubero, who passed through the area on his way to Zuni in 1697. Cubero was on the western frontier of the Kingdom of New Mexico, and like all frontier towns, it served as a point of departure for explorers, a defensive post for the military, and an active trade center

The Budville Trading Company and Scottie's Trading Post across the street provided Indian arts and crafts, food, gas, and lodging.

Cubero, once on the edge of the Spanish frontier, has weathered 300 years of change.
Photograph by Ben Wittick, ca. 1900.

that mediated exchanges between the settled Spanish Colonial and, later, Mexican towns and the nomadic people to the west, beyond the control of the government. The town, many of its houses formed either of adobe or of the same blond sandstone as the tombstones, includes ruins and near-ruins intermingled with inhabited homes and trailers. The crowded communal nature of the community resembles the clustered villages of Acoma and Laguna. The postboxes bear Hispanic surnames that duplicate those on the graves and

The Villa de Cubero Trading Post, built in 1936 in the Mediterranean Revival style, caters to a steady stream of locals from Acoma, Laguna, and Cubero. Photographed 1992.

those in the church records going back for three centuries. Like many of the oldest towns in New Mexico, the place is a study in a people's tenacity against formidable odds. Budville may have died slowly as the old highway gave way to the new, but such changes represented minor blips in the scale of change that Cubero has weathered over the past 300 years.

Back on the main track of Route 66, another group of old buildings hangs onto the road's shoulder just past Budville. In their midst, the **Villa de Cubero Trading Post** still keeps its doors open and is one of the best remaining examples of its genre along this segment of Route 66. A trader based in Cubero named S. S. Gottlieb had built his first trading company in Cubero and in 1937 moved it to the realigned highway, which bypassed the old town. The design of the Mediterranean Revival style trading post he constructed is based on plans for the original trading post at nearby Old Laguna, since modified. Gottlieb obtained the plans from his friend Sigfried Abraham, a trader at Laguna. The Mediterranean style is similar to the California Mission Revival style of architecture and no other buildings in the area, least of all those in the old village of Cubero, resemble it remotely.

Along with the main retail store at Villa de Cubero, several associated buildings remain, all of them faithful to the Mediterranean style of the trading post. The post's freestanding cabins date from the 1930s and include attached double garages, an innovation to previous hotel designs specifically tailored to accommodate automobile travelers. The Gottlieb home also stands to the rear of the store.

The "trading posts" at Villa de Cubero and Budville exemplify a common trend in the design and function of trading posts in the region as Route 66 developed. Early traders coming into the area after the Civil War and in the latter decades of the nineteenth century—many of them, like Gottlieb and Abraham, of Jewish descent—had served as middlemen for the exchange of Indian-made goods for foodstuffs and manufactured items, which the traders

NEW MEXICO ROUTE 66 ON TOUR

shipped off to markets in distant towns and cities. The advent of the railroad and then of Route 66 traffic brought tourists more directly into the equation. At the same time, many Indians were obtaining vehicles and now came to the posts for gasoline as well as supplies. As a result, the conventional "trading post" plan began to shift toward a more diversified rural service complex. Here a traveler could gas up his car while browsing through Indian arts and crafts, and the addition of a café and hotel rooms allowed him to dine and spend the night.

The retail outlets fueled an increase in the demand for local crafts as well as their less authentic, manufactured imitations, drawing Native craftspeople from Acoma, Laguna, the Navajo Reservation, and Zuni. Hispanic arts and crafts also found ready buyers at the posts, including weavers in the Spanish Colonial tradition from faraway villages such as Chimayó in Northern New Mexico. The Indians traded their pottery, rugs, and jewelry for groceries, supplies, and gasoline. The trading post often allowed travelers and Indians their only direct contact as they encountered one another at the gas pump or restaurant. Now the clientele of westward-traveling tourists is almost gone from Villa de Cubero, but the trading company caters to a steady stream of locals from Acoma, Laguna, and Cubero, who utilize it much like any modern grocery/convenience store.

A few miles beyond Villa de Cubero, Route 66 cuts directly through another old Hispanic town, **San Fidel,** originally settled in 1868 by the Jaramillo family and first named La Vega de San José. Perhaps because of its proximity to the highway, San Fidel doesn't have a half-abandoned look and lacks the old-world atmosphere of Cubero. A Catholic mission boarding school has helped the town keep some of its vitality despite the demise of Route 66. Ray's Bar is still active but all the buildings that attended Route 66 travelers—like the Acoma Curio Shop and a garage that offered auto repairs— lie dormant. A lovely white chapel bearing painted blue angels and the name "St. Joseph's Church" graces the town, built in a style typical of the many small Catholic churches that are central features of all Hispanic towns and Indian pueblos of New Mexico. The newer Pentecostal Church of God and the World of Truth Ministries in San Fidel signal the beginning of an increasing number of evangelical churches from this point westward as Route 66 penetrates more and more into places populated by the Navajo—a group of Indians that, unlike the Pueblos, was never successfully missionized by the Catholic Church and has proved a rich field for other, more recently arrived sects.

West of San Fidel, an abandoned Whiting Brothers gas station and motel mark the end of the intermittent strip of roadside businesses that began at Budville. The road veers to the south and passes under Interstate 40 and into the village of McCartys, one of the several small settlements comprised by Acoma Pueblo.

Here at McCartys, old stone homes and tiny corn fields watered by *acequias* (irrigation ditches) drawn from the Rio San José preserve an echo of traditional village life. This and the other small agricultural towns of Acoma represent the western extremity of irrigation farming that centered on the Rio Grande at the time of the Spanish arrival. With the exception of the Acomas and the dry-farming Hopi people in eastern Arizona, from this point west, the geographic norm was of nomadic people engaged in hunting, gathering, herding—and raiding—until the railroad made its way into the area.

A simple but elegant stone church perches on the talus slope of the mesa just above McCartys. Made of rock hewn from local sources, the Santa María mission blends into the landscape and escapes the notice of many passersby. John Gaw Meem designed the church in Pueblo Mission style; its contours closely resemble those of the mission atop Acoma mesa, built in 1629, and the many other Franciscan missions of Spanish Colonial New Mexico. This type of refined traditional architecture, carefully integrating Spanish and Pueblo influences, is the signature of Meem, who, along with his preservation and restoration colleagues, was responsible for the restoration of many churches in New Mexico, including the San Esteban Mission at Acoma.

West of McCartys, Route 66 winds back under the interstate, passes an old Parker Through-Truss Bridge over the San José River, skirts sandstone mesas, and cuts through the black, jagged basalt of the McCartys lava flow. This river of lava originated not from the much older flows of Mount Taylor but from a cinder cone on a broad lava shield some thirty miles to the south of the road. The McCartys flow has greatly restricted travel for centuries. Too rough for wagons and too tortuous for horses' hooves, the flow steered both prehistoric and historic travelers to the north or south. The Spanish called such terrain *mal país*, or "bad country." The builders of Route 66 diverged from the railroad tracks to bring the road across the basalt at its narrowest point—a narrow neck in the flow just five miles from Grants.

RAILROAD-BORN, ENERGY RICH AND CASH POOR: GRANTS TO THE GREAT DIVIDE

Grants sprang up at a shipping point on the AT&SF railroad, and soon subsidiaries of the AT&SF railroad platted the town, whose initial industry focused on lumbering in the nearby Zuni Mountains. The town, squeezed between lava flows and basalt cliffs, presented travelers on Route 66 heading west with the first major hotel strip since Albuquerque. The glittering lights would have reassured those too timid to try the isolation of Budville or Villa de Cubero. Many of the hotels from the 1950s are still in business. The Leisure Lodge, Western Host, Desert Sun, Franciscan, South West, Sands, Wayside, and Lava Land—all line old Route 66 just north of the railroad tracks as they roll into Grants. In name and in architectural style they all sought to lure weary vacationers on Route 66 with images of rustic, western, and southwestern charm.

The old heart of downtown Grants lies west of the strip, built up around the nexus of the old railroad depot. Here the Lux Theater and perhaps a dozen other two-story buildings line the main street—called Santa Fe Avenue as it passes through Grants—just beside the tracks, all reflecting a period of development that predated Route 66. None was designed explicitly to accommodate automobile travelers but rather to serve locals and occasional patrons from the rail cars that paused here. They doubled as roadside hotels until the Route 66-oriented auto courts and motels were developed on the available land east of downtown.

West of Grants, Highway 66 bears the name New Mexico 122 as it heads through Milan, a town that, like Grants, saw spectacular growth with the development of uranium mining in the area in the 1950s. The old highway separates widely from the interstate here, instead following the railroad tracks. About eight miles from Grants, a deep blue sign—towering fifty feet above the roadway to assure that no driver misses it—announces the pres-

GRANTS

Black Mesa

1st St.

547

Rio San Jose

TO MILAN

66

Santa Fe Ave

TO ALBUQUERQUE

40

53

Malpais (lava flow)

Route 66 through Grants, ca. 1956.

Franciscan Lodge, Grants.
Photograph by Don Usner, 2001.

ence of the Bluewater Inn, long closed up and hosting only rodents and the wind. This would have been a beacon for travelers, and still there is nothing to compete with this lonely outpost on a straight stretch of empty road. It drew its name from the nearby settlement of Bluewater, a farming town founded by Mormons in the 1890s, originally called Mormontown. The first settlers built an earth dam on Bluewater Creek, impounding the water for extensive agricultural land, but bigger farms in California dried up the farmers' corner on the market and Bluewater Lake now has become a popular recreation site.

Beyond the Bluewater Inn, a string of widely separated trading posts along old Route 66 would have presented the only potential stops for supplies and refueling for many miles. The first, an abandoned whitewashed building with its lettered name faded beyond recognition, now blends into the golden grasslands. A mere half-mile beyond, the long-shut Rattlesnake Trading Post is only in slightly better repair, and then it's five miles to the small town of Prewitt and the Prewitt Trading Post, where the lettering and exterior bear few indications that this is any more active than any other abandoned stores along the route. This, however, is one of the few old posts that still does business. The interior's chaotic mix of basic groceries with all sorts of dusty odds and ends primarily serves local Navajo people, and still offers to pawn jewelry in exchange for supplies.

Prewitt was originally settled by Hispanic ranchers who called the settlement "Baca." The new name slowly replaced the old starting in 1916, when Harold Prewitt founded a trading post in the town. Prewitt's trading post served as a supply point for logging camps in the nearby Zuni Mountains, where massive timbering was taking place to provide ties for the expanding AT&SF railroad. Prewitt's later sheep ranching operation became the focal point of the regional economy. Today, many Navajos are drawn to Prewitt because of employment opportunities at the coal-powered generating station, visible to the north but absent during Route 66's heyday.

By now, the route has entered into country mostly populated by Navajo people (although still outside the boundaries of the Navajo Reservation) and the first hogans—traditional Navajo homes, rounded in shape and often made of logs—appear near the road, all of them situated alongside more modern homes that serve as current residences. Each of the widely scattered hogans with its attendant woodpile and corrals represents a single matriarchal lineage—an arrangement that contrasts sharply with the tightly clustered, easily defended settlements of the Pueblo people and their Hispanic neighbors back in the San José and Rio Grande valleys. Whereas the traditional Pueblo housing reflects the communal societies of closely integrated groups, Navajo homes typically reflect a pastoral lifestyle that required that each extended family retain large open spaces for grazing. The distinctive building plan of hogans presents design and construction challenges that have limited its adaptation in modern buildings. Unlike the Pueblo and Spanish design elements seen ubiquitously in architecture of the Southwest, very few structures imitate hogans. The Gallup Chamber of Commerce built its headquarters in the shape of a cluster of hogans in the 1930s, but these were since demolished.

As Mount Taylor diminishes in size to the east, deep red cliffs of Wingate sandstone come into view here, the first landforms to make obvious the landscape's connection to the well-known mesa lands in the heart of the Colorado Plateau. The rising elevation of the road becomes apparent as well, as the piñon-juniper woodlands become thicker, the air thinner and cooler. More than any other landscape encountered thus far on Route 66, the views here would have struck travelers in the 1930s and '40s as the quintessential "western" landscape, largely because of the widely popular movies made there during the very decades that Route 66 was most traveled.

The Red Mountain Market and Deli and Johnnie's Inn mark the crossroads with NM 371, which heads north to Thoreau and on for seventy miles to Chaco Canyon—the most spectacular and well known of the countless prehistoric ruins that litter the region. Thoreau began as a shipping point on the AT&SF and, like all railroad towns, is strung out along the tracks of the railroad just north of Route 66. Like so many towns on the margins of the Hispanic homeland, this place originally bore a Hispanic name—Cháves—to recognize a prominent and long-established family there. Then came the railroad and entrepreneurs who began lumbering in the Zuni Mountains and laid out a townsite called Mitchell. Still later, the railroad stop at Mitchell became the supply point for the Hyde Exploring Expedition, an organization that was excavating at Chaco Canyon and renamed the locale in honor of the philosopher Henry David Thoreau.

From the Thoreau turnoff Route 66, distant from the roar of I-40, continues its slow climb toward the Continental Divide, passing the Thunderbird

Trading Company and angling closer to the rich red cliffs of Wingate sandstone to the north. At the Divide, a cluster of "trading posts" appears, most of them still active and all advertised with garishly painted false facades like wild West movie sets—a building style divergent from others in this segment of Route 66 but typical of many trading posts and curio shops elsewhere in New Mexico.

The Continental Divide, at 7,263 feet in elevation, marks the highest point on Route 66 in New Mexico or anywhere along its 2,400-mile length. Here the road leaves the drainage of the San José River, which it has shadowed since leaving the Rio Grande, and begins a slow descent of the Rio Puerco of the West, whose destination is the Colorado River and finally the Gulf of California. This represents a cultural divide also. From here on, churches built by the Church of Latter-day Saints (Mormons) become more and more common, Spanish and Mexican influences begin to decline and Navajos outnumber other ethnicities. Architectural elements likewise shift away from southwestern motifs. The cultural worlds of Arizona and California begin to pull more strongly than the Hispanic and Pueblo heartland of New Mexico.

The rich energy resources of the Colorado Plateau, glimpsed in the coal plant at Prewitt and the closed uranium mines at Grants, become apparent again just past the divide, where Route 66 and I-40 coincide and come upon an oil refinery adjacent to a Giant Superstore. This modern-day service complex on I-40 serves many of the same purposes as Route 66 trading posts but completely dwarfs anything from that era. A few miles beyond the divide an exit to Iyanbito leads to another segment of Route 66. Just beyond, a turnoff to Fort Wingate branches off to the south from Route 66.

Amid modern occupied buildings, many old structures remain at Fort Wingate from its several reincarnations since it began as an army outpost named Fort Fauntleroy in 1860. The U.S. Army, which had only recently annexed the New Mexico Territory, situated the fort at the base of the Zuni Mountains, a longtime campsite for Navajos, who called the place *Shush bi toh* (Bear Springs). In building this and several other forts, the army sought to control the Navajos and to secure the emerging east-west travel routes across the territory to newly discovered goldfields in California.

The army hastily renamed the site Fort Lyon when its namesake defected to the Confederate Army in 1861 but then abandoned the fort and built the first Fort Wingate at a site some sixty miles away, near San Rafael. The Navajo people were completely subjugated and marched to Bosque Redondo on the Pecos River in 1864 on their infamous Long Walk, during which many died and all suffered greatly. The experiment in turning Navajo herdsmen and raiders into farmers failed and in 1868 the government decided to return the Navajos to their homeland and to designate for them a reservation. Fort

Wingate was reestablished on the old site to help assure the Navajos' submission and to maintain order on the new reservation.

The army abandoned Fort Wingate again in 1911, reoccupied it as a detention center for 4,000 Mexican Army refugees from the Pancho Villa revolt in Sonora, Mexico, then left it again in 1918. A new facility, the Fort Wingate Ordinance Depot, was established a few miles to the northwest and in 1925 the old fort became property of the Indian Bureau, to be used as a boarding school. The Indian Bureau, later the Bureau of Indian Affairs, razed many of the old adobe buildings of the fort to make room for dormitories and classrooms. Since 1968, the remaining buildings from the fort, most of them made of stone and rough-hewn timbers, have been abandoned and boarded up.

The fort now houses one of the few remaining Navajo boarding schools as well as a day high school, but it retains the feeling of an old fort in layout and in some historic architecture. Although only one major building from the nineteenth-century remains, all newer buildings have been placed around the original parade grounds, including one barracks, several homes from the turn of the century and many of the original boarding school structures. Military burials from the fort were removed to Santa Fe for reburial in 1915 but the fort's original cemetery is still in use for interring Navajo veterans. There one finds graves of Mexican soldiers who died during their stay at the fort.

Other parts of Fort Wingate have also continued to find new purposes as times change. The ordnance depot was decommissioned in 1993 and it has become a Missile Launch Complex for the Ballistic Missile Defense Organization, administered by the Department of Energy. The rows and rows of subterranean bunkers, called igloos, used to shelter munitions. They now lie dormant, although recent proposals have suggested utilizing them to store archaeological artifacts, which would be well preserved in the cool, uniform temperatures of the bunkers.

Route 66 continues westward from the Fort Wingate turnoff, passing by Red Rock State Park as it approaches Gallup. The park is the site of the annual Intertribal Indian Ceremonial, the largest gathering of Native people in the U.S. Begun in Gallup in 1922, the ceremonial used to take place closer to town but was relocated to make way for the construction of Interstate 40.

A hogback—one of many anticlines (tilted blocks of rock) common on the Colorado Plateau—stretches north-south for ten miles just east of Gallup, creating a formidable barrier to east-west traffic. Early trails and roadways, the railroad, Route 66, and now I-40—as well as power, phone, and gas lines—all aim for a narrow break in the hogback. Gallup's commercial strip begins at the narrow notch in the hogback and stretches for some thirteen miles along old Route 66, paralleled by I-40 just to the north.

Gallup has been a hub for regional trade and development since its founding in 1881 as a maintenance center and re-coaling stop for trains. It soon became a booming coal-mining town serving the railroad as well as smelters in Arizona. As the primary supply point for the vast Navajo Reservation, Gallup developed a robust mercantile economy. Wagons rolled out of Gallup daily, destined for trading posts throughout the reservation and beyond. It was the largest trading center in the West for Indian-made goods—a fact that was not lost on railroad developers intent on promoting tourism. Soon, Gallup became known as the Indian capital of the West.

Gallup's Chamber of Commerce was inspired by Navajo prototypes. Photograph by W. T. Mullarky.

Gas stations and motels catering to travelers line Route 66 as soon as it enters Gallup from the east, but most of them date from the few decades that have elapsed since the construction of I-40. An older motel row, built in the 1950s and '60s, begins just a mile and change east of downtown Gallup, deliberately clustered near the **El Rancho**—the first motel on the strip and perennially the most well known. With Route 66 traffic increasing exponentially, the old two-story hotels of downtown and the later auto camps on Coal Avenue lost their appeal when compared to the modern new motels, which offered convenient parking, modern rooms, and access to new restaurants and gas stations. In architectural detail, the motels on the strip also offered western and southwestern lures. The El Capitán, the Arrowhead, the Blue Spruce, the Lariat, the Zia, the Redwood, the Coronado—all sought to capitalize on a kind of rustic western traveler mystique while at the same time offering modern conveniences. The motto of the El Rancho embodied this creed: "The Charm of Yesterday and the Convenience of Tomorrow."

The El Rancho was built during a building surge in the 1930s and '40s, when hotels and motels of the downtown strips along Route 66 and Coal Avenue in downtown Gallup proved unable to handle the increasing numbers of tourists. It was the first hotel to step out of the bounds of Gallup and was conceived by the movie director R. E. "Griff" Griffith, who had fallen in love with Gallup and had initiated the makeover of the Chief Theater downtown. About the same time that the El Rancho made its debut, the Intertribal Indian Ceremonial was gaining in popularity, and many of those attending chose to stay at the El Rancho, located across the street from the grounds where the event took place. The hotel also became the primary lodging and social club for the movie industry's many out-of-town actors and other employees—and a popular, illicit gambling spot and watering hole for high-society locals. Hundreds of movie stars have stayed at the El Rancho, and the celebrity atmosphere of the hotel endured for decades.

In keeping with Gallup's emerging reputation as a rustic, western town—an image more reflective of Hollywood's fancy rather than Gallup's reality—Griffith invented a rambling, ranch style building with a picturesque western look. Most of the hotels that followed the El Rancho to form a new hotel strip in the 1940s and '50s incorporated elements of western and southwestern styling to varying degrees, but none took it to the extremes of El Rancho. The El Rancho fully embraced an architectural style that came to be known as the Rustic style, and it is the only building to truly fit this genre in Gallup.

For building materials, the El Rancho combines brick, random ashlar stone, and rough-hewn wood. Some of the brick was laid in an irregular, wavy pattern to enhance the hotel's rustic fantasy appearance. The central three-story building, built of randomly laid ashlar stone, includes the lobby and the oldest rooms. Brick and stone chimneys protrude from the second-story's pitched, wood-shake roof. Walls of both stories are painted white and dark brown. A large portico over the first-floor entrance—an odd appurtenance that brings to mind the pretentious grandeur of the southern plantation home—is supported by wooden beams and holds up a second-story balcony.

Each of the three main ground-floor entry doors is made of rough-hewn wood and contains a rounded porthole-like window. The doors open into the large, square lobby, dimly lit and further darkened by a prevalence of stained woodwork throughout the interior. Vertical posts made of pine logs support a

Gallup's El Rancho was the quintessential "western" hotel. Its gracious rooms, named after the movie stars who stayed there, still serve a multitude of tourists eager to visit Indian Country.
Don Usner, 2001.

crisscross, wooden balustrade balcony that runs around the perimeter of the second-story level; Navajo rugs drape its railing. Two wooden stairways with treads of split logs laid flat side up wind their way up to the balcony on either side of a massive stone fireplace. Naturally bent, stripped and polished tree limbs form the stairways' railings. Countless portraits of the movie stars who have stayed at the El Rancho peer from the upstairs walls, while mounted heads of game animals stare from walls on the ground floor. Heavy, dark, carved wood furniture circles a central area covered with cowhide rugs and faintly lit by stamped tin lamps. One architect succinctly described the ambience of this spacious lobby as "rusticated western grandeur mixed with the feeling of a hunting lodge."

East and west wings and other additions have been added to the El Rancho's central building over subsequent decades, all adhering to the look of the original structure. For nearly three decades, the El Rancho was the place to be and to be seen in Gallup, but gradually its popularity faded. In the late 1980s management filed for bankruptcy and the premises were sold at auction to Indian trader Armand Ortega, who renovated the building to restore it to something of its former glory.

BRICK BLOCKS ALONG TWIN STREETS: DOWNTOWN GALLUP

Because Gallup sprang up as a railroad town, its downtown began as a few businesses along the street in front of the train depot and quickly grew into a thriving commercial district of false-front banks, mercantile stores, and saloons. The nascent roadway was known as "Railroad Avenue." When Route 66 was routed through Gallup in 1926, it paralleled the tracks into town but then took a detour away from Railroad Avenue to follow the adjacent, recently developed thoroughfare of Coal Avenue, then assumed its place alongside the rails as it headed west. A gradual process of relocating the rails to make room for the highway finally allowed for a straightening of Route 66 through town in 1939, but by then the two-thoroughfare downtown district was well established.

The two parallel streets—Coal Avenue and Route 66—still form the heart of town. Newer hotels and other businesses oriented toward highway travelers stretched out to the east and west in later decades as Route 66 brought increasing numbers of visitors. The entire downtown district is remarkably well preserved and gives a sense of the town's appearance in the days when the railroad and the coal mines drove a vibrant local economy. Most of the buildings are still in use and support flourishing businesses based on Gallup's continuing role as a regional trade center and supply point for the Navajo Reservation.

The familiar-looking, two-story brick buildings of downtown Gallup appear just a mile beyond the El Rancho—familiar because they look like turn-of-the-century downtown buildings from anywhere in the USA. Although impressive for its state of preservation, Gallup's downtown district at first glance offers little architecturally to distinguish it from countless others of the era. The ubiquitous use of light colored Gallup brick lends some distinction, but most of the unaltered, historic structures in town are utilitarian, brick or stone business blocks, stores, offices, and hotels—a style dubbed Decorative Brick Commercial—and are the work of builders/designers without formal architectural training. A closer look at Gallup, however, reveals diverse architectural styles derived from Route 66 and railroad days as well as a time that might be called the movie-making era in Gallup. Architectural gems are tucked away here and there amid the clustered brick constructs of downtown.

Perhaps the most impressive bit of architecture, however, lies just a few blocks east of the brick mélange by the tracks. The still-active **McKinley County Courthouse**, a massive, four-story building, is one of only a handful of buildings in Gallup that represent a major architectural expression. The renowned El Paso architectural firm Trost and Trost designed the Pueblo Revival style courthouse, which was built in the waning years of the Great Depression with Works Progress Administration Funds and decorated inside with murals, paintings, and furniture by WPA artists. The courthouse towers an impressive four stories high, with additional elevation coming from an eight-foot parapet and a ten-foot-tall bell tower.

McKinley County
Courthouse, Gallup.
Photograph by Don Usner, 2001.

Vigas protrude from the courthouse's brown stucco walls, which also bear some painted wood features. Inside, painted wood beams, posts, and corbels embellish the ground floor and a stepped parapet ornaments the upper walls.

In keeping with Gallup's reputation as a center for Indian arts, Indian motifs dominate the interior décor—in the stucco reliefs that flank the main entry, in the tile wainscoting at the base of the plaster walls, and in the lettered signs and paintings on the walls. Many wall paintings replicate designs derived from Navajo sand paintings. The heavy emphasis on Indian motifs extends even to the pendant light fixtures that hang from the lobby ceiling.

WPA-era paintings hang in offices throughout the courthouse, bearing now-famous names such as W.E. Rollins, Helmuth Naumer, Anna K. Wilton, Fremont Ellis, and others. Some wall paintings were adapted from originals located in the El Navajo Hotel, since demolished. A panoramic mural completed in the 1940s by Lloyd Moylan—the largest remaining WPA-commissioned artwork in New Mexico—sweeps around the walls of the main courtroom on the second floor, depicting the history of the region from the very origins of life in Paleozoic seas through the arrival of the railroad. A bit of more recent history is preserved in the wooden jury box, which bears two ragged bullet holes dating from a courtroom dispute in the 1950s.

The **Atchison, Topeka, and Santa Fe Railway Depot** predated and once rivaled the courthouse in stature and architectural design, but its grandeur was diminished when the attached **El Navajo Hotel** was demolished in 1958 to make room for a parking lot. The unified hotel/depot structure was designed in 1916 (although construction was delayed by World War I until 1923) by Mary Colter, one of the Southwest's most influential and prolific architects of the turn of the century. Colter conceived the building with strong elements of early modern styling, making it one of the first AT&SF railroad terminals to diverge from the Pueblo Revival style. The building no doubt influenced Trost and Trost in their plan for the courthouse.

The Atchison, Topeka, and Santa Fe Railway Depot and adjacent El Navajo Hotel were designed in 1916 by Mary Colter, one of the Southwest's most influential and prolific architects at the turn of the century. The depot was remodeled in the past decade and continues to serve as a transportation hub and business center. The hotel was demolished in 1958 to create the parking lot.

Colter was an employee of the Fred Harvey Company, which was responsible for planning the hotel and depot structures for the AT&SF Railway and also devised and promoted Indian Country Tours. Colter is best known for designing the most prominent buildings at Grand Canyon National Park, but she also designed numerous important railway stations throughout the Southwest.

The Gallup Depot/El Navajo Hotel was Colter's first project as chief designer for Fred Harvey. In departing from the previous use of Pueblo Revival and Mission styling, Colter sought to pay tribute to Native Americans and to blend ancient and modern architecture into one unified style. This groundbreaking departure from previous styles helped establish Colter's standing as a major figure in southwestern architecture. One of Colter's special touches was expressed in the layout and décor of interiors. She used Navajo rugs, Pueblo pottery, and leather furniture as well as Art Deco lighting fixtures to blend old and new, traditional and innovative. Her use of Navajo sand painting symbols on the walls of the hotel marked the first time permission was given for these images to be reproduced. Nearly two thousand Native Americans attended the building's grand opening, including some of the oldest medicine men from the Navajo Nation.

The depot was renovated and remodeled to make a transportation center and exhibit space in the 1990s, and many of the original details have been masked by newer innovations. Nevertheless, as the only structure in Gallup still in use and directly related to the arrival of the railroad, the building represents an important milestone in the history of Gallup and the region.

The Old **U.S. Post Office** building at 1st and Coal, built in 1933, was the first WPA project in New Mexico. Like the courthouse and rail depot, it shows careful architectural planning, but its designers juxtaposed a number of styles. The result is a handsome and unusual building that stands out in Gallup, although it lacks the regional distinctions of the courthouse and the depot.

The former United States Post Office building at 1st and Coal was the first WPA project in New Mexico. A mixture of Mediterranean Revival styles on the outside, the interior walls were decorated with wall murals representing Indian themes.
Photograph taken during construction, 1933–34

The center section of the four-part building is dominated by a large, Mediterranean-style tiled roof coupled with a tall, Pueblo Revival portal. In keeping with the regional styling, the portal's concrete columns are capped with wood corbels and beams painted in several colors, but the two flights of stairs leading to the entrance to the lobby are bordered by Mediterranean-style balustrades.

In contrast to the central portion of the building, the tall, rectangular east and west wings of the building are styled similarly to the older decorative brick buildings of the downtown district, with the addition of governmental-style shield details. The rectangular, flat-roofed, two-story back of the building also utilizes exposed brick. Its main feature is a loading dock covered by an impressive suspended copper overhang, probably originally serving as a porch.

In keeping with the civic architecture of the day, the focus of the post office's interior design is the lobby, where fifteen-foot-high ceilings and a large floor plan lend an atmosphere of grandeur and authority. The tiles, fixtures, woodwork, and trim details came from artists throughout New Mexico. The walls were decorated with murals based on Indian themes akin to those found in the courthouse, but these have been lost in remodeling over the years. The mosaic red clay tile floor is still intact, as are the large carved eagles beneath the ceiling beams.

The old post office, the courthouse, and the railway station are exceptions to the brick rule in downtown Gallup, but some more conventional brick buildings incorporated modest but still striking design elements to distinguish them from other structures. The **White Café**, built around 1928 on Route 66, is the most ornate of these. The café was built before the Great Depression and during Gallup's second major coal-related economic boom and its first automobile-related boom. It was a favorite stopping point for travelers before the more modern and specifically automobile-oriented motels sprang up on

Gallup's White Café, built around 1928, represents the more conventional side of Route 66 architecture. Photograph by J. R. Willis, ca. 1929.

El Morro Theatre occupies a prominent location on old Route 66 and for decades has been the backdrop for many Gallup Intertribal Ceremonial parades. Built in 1928, it is the only Spanish Eclectic architecture represented in Gallup.
Photograph by J. R. Willis, ca. 1930

Coal Avenue and then east of downtown. Many Route 66 travelers stayed overnight in the White Café's upstairs rooms. The café billed itself "the traveler's headquarters" and provided free road maps to patrons.

Unlike many other buildings downtown, the White Café building has never been stuccoed and the whimsical brickwork is still visible. Builders used dark red, glazed brick to highlight a background of blond brick, placing large, geometric designs between the first and second stories. The top of the café is lined with a parapet cap made of glazed red brick, which is in turn highlighted by a stylistic row of glazed red brick below. Dark red-glazed brick arches above and soldier course sills below also boldly highlight second-story windows. The unusual corner entrance door at the café's east corner and part of the original White Café sign still remain, the sign placed conspicuously high on the second story to be visible to people stepping off the train at the railroad depot down the street.

A block south of Route 66 on Coal Avenue, two theaters stand out even more starkly than the White Café as departures from the brick commercial styles of downtown. Architecturally, the **El Morro and Chief theaters** couldn't be more different from each other or from other structures on the street. Each one is a unique representative of its own style in Gallup.

The Chief Theater on Coal Avenue has undergone significant remodeling and a change in name (to the City Electric Shoe Shop) since its construction as the Strand Theater in 1920. The original structure was remodeled with Art Deco design highlighted with Egyptian motifs in the early 1920s. The theater received a face-lift and a name change in 1936, when a new façade was added to the building. The new structure still reflected the popular Art Deco styles prevailing at the time, but here the theme was given a distinctly southwestern twist: the vertical string courses on the second story are lined with zigzag relief ornamentation emulating Native American patterns found on weaving and basketry, and the use of bright red and turquoise colors to highlight this plaster ornamentation alludes to the turquoise stone and red coral in Navajo and Pueblo jewelry. This peculiar regionalization of Art Deco has been called Pueblo Deco and is not found outside of New Mexico, Arizona, and Texas. The Chief Theater is the only example of the style in Gallup.

The former Strand Theater, now a retail business, originally featured an Art Deco–styled façade decorated in Egyptian motifs. Originally constructed in 1920, the building was changed in 1936 to include Pueblo Deco elements and re-named the Chief Theater. The current building retains some Pueblo Deco features.
Photograph by W. T. Mullarky, ca. 1936

The Chief gained notoriety in its day because of its association with luminaries of the movie industry, which inundated Gallup with Hollywood personalities and money. Among these was director R. E. Griffith, who came to Gallup to direct a movie in the early 1930s and later returned to build the El Rancho Hotel. The striking new Pueblo Deco façade of the theater was added under Griffith's direction in 1936.

The El Morro Theater also made an architectural statement when it opened just down the street from the Strand Theater (later the Chief Theater) in 1928. The businessmen of the Gallup Realty Company who financed the building engaged Carl Boller, an architect from Los Angeles—well known today in New Mexico as the designer of the KiMo Theater in Albuquerque—to design the exterior. The Boller Brothers firm designed more than ninety theaters in the Midwest, Southwest, and

California, and its architects planned the Gallup building in the Spanish Colonial Revival style—a building style more typical of California than New Mexico. The theater's promoters declared that the El Morro would be a place "where you could hear music that would entrance and delight you, and where novelty entertainment would reign supreme." They embraced the exotic and expensive Spanish Colonial style with the expectation that its popularity would bring a return on their investment. They weren't disappointed, as from its inception the El Morro was a mainstay of the entertainment life of Gallup.

The renovated, two-story El Morro—the only Spanish Eclectic style building in Gallup—is still in use and shows off many of the original design details. The ornate central façade is the centerpiece of the building plan and bears classic elements of the Spanish Colonial style, including arched windows; ornate, molded, half-round columns; molded shields; porthole-like openings with molded plaster trim; and a decorative, molded plaster parapet with molded shields. A parapet capped with clay tile tops the barrel-vault roof of the building.

Storefronts on either side of the theater flank a recessed entrance foyer that leads to the original ticket office, decorated with glazed tile in a zigzag pattern. The original poster display cases, also with zigzagging tile, are also still in use. The exterior maroon ceramic tiles became a symbol of modernization throughout Gallup's business district as other building owners incorporated them in renovations over the following decades.

Inside the El Morro Theater, a rectangular lobby and snack bar lead to the theater, where rows of seats slope to the stage and stairs rise to a balcony, now not in use. Originally, the stage was surrounded by a large Reuters organ used for silent movies and vaudeville, and a "cry room" adjoined the ladies' room. The walls of the theater were lavishly decorated with murals painted by David A. Swing of Phoenix, that depicted locally important historical scenes, with titles such as "Oñate Passing El Morro," "Surrender of the Zunis to Coronado," and "Pioneers Passing Church Rock." Unfortunately, the murals have been painted over.

On the western side of downtown, just west of the commercial strip, the **Log Cabin Lodge** utilized rustic styling to create a fantasy of western ambience, although it did so on a much more modest scale than the El Rancho. When it was built in the 1930s, it was the first motel that eastbound travelers encountered upon entering Gallup. Its freestanding cabins included attached or detached garages alongside the cabins. By presenting the image of a cozy mountain cabin, the owners sought to be the first in Gallup to snag motorists who had been driving across the searing expanses of Arizona for hours, if not days. Individual cabins offered wood or coal-burning stoves or stone fireplaces to take off the winter chill and covered porches—ringed by low log railings, of course—for shelter from the scorching summer sun. In a scaled-down version of the El Rancho, a large central lobby sported game trophies and Navajo rugs to create a homey western atmosphere.

The Log Cabin Lodge's nine rustic-style cabins are arranged in two parallel lines facing each other to create a courtyard, with a post-and-pole framed garage at the rear—one of the best examples remaining along Route 66 in New Mexico of a pre–World War II tourist court. Logs for the cabins came from the pine forests of the nearby Continental Divide, and tourists on Route 66 were clamoring for rooms there before steps to the porches were complete. The office northeast of the rooms utilizes the same materials and style as the cabins, but a newer portion to the east of the office and two-story motel building to the rear have flat roofs and white walls and employ some elements of Southwest Vernacular style.

West of the Log Cabin Lodge, Route 66 continues past a seemingly endless strip of roadside motels and other businesses, all of them of a more modern vintage than those downtown and farther east. Eventually, however, Gallup ends and Route 66 resumes its lonely ramble through the dust-bitten mesa lands of the Colorado Plateau—a part of New Mexico that is almost wholly occupied by Navajo people and only a few miles from the border of "the Rez." The westernmost stretch of Route 66 in New Mexico winds above the eroded chasm of the Rio Puerco of the West. It passes numerous Navajo hogans, sometimes cruising right up against the base of the stunning sandstone cliffs on the valley's north side to avoid the shifting sands of the floodplain. Finally reaching the Arizona border it leaves New Mexico at the biggest tourist trap along its entire 300-mile sojourn in the state, where the Indian Market, Fort Yellow Horse, and the Chaparral, Chief and Teepee Trading Posts crowd for space along the cliffs, decorated on upper ledges with a miniature bestiary of elk, deer, and other animals. A few abandoned Route 66 businesses sit crumbling under Chinese elms across the way, marking the exit of the state much as the abandoned structures stood guard at Glenrio on the state's eastern border.

SUGGESTED READING

Bunting, Bainbridge. *Of Earth and Timbers Made: New Mexico Architecture*.
Albuquerque: University of New Mexico Press, 1974.

Julyan, Robert. *The Place Names of New Mexico*, rev. ed. Albuquerque: University of
New Mexico Press, 1998.

Kessell, John L. *Kiva, Cross, and Crown: The Pecos Indians and New Mexico
1540–1840*. Albuquerque: University of New Mexico Press, 1987.

Noble, David Grant. *Pueblos, Villages, Forts and Trails: A Guide to New Mexico's
Past*. Albuquerque: University of New Mexico Press, 1994.

Noe, Sally. *Greetings from Gallup: Six Decades of Route 66*. Gallup: Gallup
Downtown Development Corporation, 1991.

Nostrand, Richard L. *The Hispano Homeland*. Norman: University of Oklahoma
Press, 1992.

Ortiz, Alfonso (vol. ed.). *Handbook of North American Indians, Volume 9:
Southwest*. Washington, D.C.: Smithsonian Institution, 1979.

Scott, Quinta. *Along Route 66*. Norman: University of Oklahoma Press, 2000.

Spears, Beverly. *American Adobes: Rural Houses of Northern New Mexico*.
Albuquerque: University of New Mexico Press, 1986.

Williams, Jerry L. (ed.). *New Mexico in Maps* (2nd ed.). Albuquerque:
University of New Mexico Press, 1986

Wilson, Chris. *The Myth of Santa Fe: Creating a Modern Regional Tradition*.
Albuquerque: University of New Mexico Press, 1997.

Photo Credits

AM (Albuquerque Museum); HPD (New Mexico Historic Preservation Division); MNM (Museum of New Mexico Photo Archives); SRCA (State Records Center and Archives). Photos 2, 6, 7, 9, 12, 13, 17, 19, 26, 48, 50, 56, 59, 87 (top), 88 courtesy HPD. Photos 4 (top) MNM174713; 4 (bottom) MNM46637; 10 MNM46637; 25 MNM9777; 31 MNM177663; 32 MNM40290; 33 MNM; 35 MNM12986; 37 MNM; 38 MNM59349; 39 MNM 14866; 46 MNM59108; 49 MNM512; 66 (top) mnm71406; 69 MNM177584; 81 MNM59086; 87 (bottom) MNM15758; 91 MNM56395; 92 MNM88912; 101 MNM150084; 102 MNM152350. Photo 40 (top) AM,1981.047.001; 40 (bottom) AM,1990.013.131 museum purchase; 61 AM, Alb. Progress Collection; 63 AM,1990.059.015, gift of Jones Family; 64 AM,1996.059.013; 66 (bottom) AM,1982.180.255, Ward Hicks Collection, gift of John Airy; 68 AM,1978.152.223, gift of Channell Graham and Harold Brooks; 69 AM,1975.063.648, gift of McCanna Family; 73 (top) AM,1978.151.506, gift of Channell Graham and Harold Brooks; 73 (bottom) AM,1982.180.718, Ward Hicks Collection, gift of John Airy; 76 AM,1980.185.257, Alb. Progress Collection, gift of Bank of America; 77 AM,1975.063.856. Photo frontis, SRCA7511, NM Dept. of tourism Collection; 51, SRCA38521, McDonald Collection; 54, SRCA38210, Francis Wilson Collection. Photo 27 National Park Service, 8/67/849. Photo 71 David Kammer Collection. Photos 103, 104 Collection of Walter Haussamen. Photo 105 Mullarky Camera Shop, Gallup.